Designing Successful Grant Proposals

Donald C. Orlich

Association for Supervision
and Curriculum Development
Alexandria, Virginia

Association for Supervision and Curriculum Development
1250 N. Pitt Street • Alexandria, Virginia 22314
Telephone: (703) 549-9110 • Fax: (703) 299-8631

Gene R. Carter, *Executive Director*
Michelle Terry, *Assistant Executive Director, Program Development*
Ronald S. Brandt, *Assistant Executive Director*
Nancy Modrak, *Managing Editor, ASCD Books*
Stephanie Justen, *Assistant Editor*
Gary Bloom, *Manager, Design and Production Services*
Tracey Smith, *Print Production Coordinator*
Valerie Sprague, *Desktop Publisher*

ASCD publications present a variety of viewpoints. The views expressed or
implied in this book should not be interpreted as official positions of the
Association.

Printed in the United States of America.

ASCD Stock No. 196022
P5/96
$16.95

Library of Congress Cataloging-in-Publication Data

Orlich, Donald C.
    Designing successful grant proposals / Donald C. Orlich.
        p. cm.
    Includes bibliographical references.
    ISBN 0-87120-264-6
    1. Proposal writing in education. 2. Proposal writing for grants.
I. Title.
LB2342.O75 1996
379.1'2—dc20   96-9962
                                      CIP

00 99 98 97 96   5 4 3 2 1

Designing Successful Grant Proposals

Acknowledgments

I wish to acknowledge Donald F. Kline and Gordon McCloskey for teaching me the *real ropes* of grant swinging. A special thanks goes to my long-time collaborators who crafted the winning proposals—Robert J. Harder, Jack C. Horne, and David R. Stronck. Special assistance in writing this book came from Patricia Orlich. The entire staff of the Office of Grants and Research and Development at Washington State University, especially Matt Ronning and Renee Gralewicz, gave great support and technical guidance. A note of appreciation is extended to Sandra L. Tyacke who prepared the final manuscript and to Marilyn Riebe who edited it. While the book shows an orientation to education-related proposals, the general format and content are applicable to all grant proposals. The elements developed in the eight chapters are those required for the vast majority of competitive funding announcements. At the end of each chapter are checklists that will aid all writers in improving the quality of their proposals.

DONALD C. ORLICH
Pullman, Washington

1
Organizing Your Ideas

YOU CAN BE A SUCCESSFUL GRANT PROPOSAL WRITER IF YOU FOLLOW three rather simple steps: (1) start with a good idea; (2) locate a source that has already funded similar ideas; and (3) design, craft, and develop your idea into a well-written statement. Notice the emphasis on *well written*. Successful grant-getters are those who carefully prepare their proposals, not those who just crank them out. And now that we have the basics established, how do you go about this process in an organized and business-like manner?

One assumption underlying this book is that you will write proposals for some time into the future. That is, you will become one of the thousands who continuously writes grant proposals as a regular part of your job. The process becomes a journey rather than a singular event. Since getting there is half the fun, you need to develop a systematic process of knowing what is being funded, who is willing to fund your proposals, and how to find this information.

Some Basic Elements

Virtually all agencies, foundations, or businesses require the same generic elements. The exact details may vary, but the basic elements tend to be similar whether it is a multimillion dollar proposal to the National Science Foundation or a $500 proposal to the local utility company. Let us briefly explore those elements and then spend the remaining chapters expanding each section.

1

The Introduction

Every proposal begins with a grabber, an introduction that sets the stage for the remainder of the proposal. Remember, you are communicating your ideas through a one-way medium—writing. The best proposals—make that the best written proposals—get funded in nearly every competition. Therefore, you need to spend a great deal of time and effort carefully selecting the exact wording. Every word or sentence must carry an explicit connotation and explicit denotation. Sloppiness in writing yields only rejection letters. You will spend a good deal of time preparing your proposal, so do it right.

A Need or Problem

The second basic element for all proposals is to identify the need being addressed or the problem being solved. If you address a need, you will have to provide data to support it. Chapter 3 provides a tested approach to identifying needs and conducting a needs assessment. The need statement of a proposal is best concluded with a statement of significance. Just how significant is this proposal to the group on which you are focusing the proposed efforts? Don't be modest. If it is intergalactic in nature, point that out. Keep in mind you will probably be writing your proposal to an unknown evaluation panel. Most likely, none of the panel members will know you or your institution, so you must provide instant rapport in the first two sections.

Goals and Objectives

List your goal statement next. It is current vogue to incorporate a vision statement that tends to be stated in broad, global terms. Vision statements differ as you will see later in Chapter 4. These are followed by a listing of the exact objectives that you intend to accomplish as a consequence of being funded.

Procedures

The body of the proposal or the narrative section follows your goals and objectives. This section may be called procedures, methodology, activities, or the work plan. Whatever it is called in the guidelines you'll be following, it really means providing details, details, and more details. In this section you elaborate how each objective will be attained. You answer the five W's—who, what, when, where, and why. Typically, in the procedures section, you will list how the project is organized as well as the instructional or research team members.

Evaluation

The fifth basic element of a proposal is usually the evaluation model that you will employ. The basic idea of evaluating a project is to determine how well and to what extent you successfully met the project's objectives. Chapter 5 discusses evaluation and management plans in detail.

Budget

Next is the budget. This section provides a general expenditure (investment) plan and is followed by specific details on how the general costs were determined. The latter are known as "budget justifications" and are not equivalent to the budget figures or numbers.

Basically, that is all that there is to it. In nearly all cases, the funder provides a general set of guidelines that specifies the order that these basic elements will be written. *Always follow the guidelines!* No matter how redundant or even silly you may think a set of guidelines may be, you must follow them—reviewers of your proposal will. If you deviate from the guidelines, you'll be penalized and, more than likely, not funded. It is their money, so follow their directions with the utmost care.

Communicating Your Intentions

When writing, crafting, developing, and preparing a grant proposal, communicate your intentions in such a manner that they cannot be misinterpreted by the proposal reviewers. For the most part, review panels are comprised of people just like yourself. They are typically selected to provide a wide spectrum of experiences and backgrounds.

Write explicitly so that they do not have to interpret your intentions.

Using the Problem as a Guide

The careful crafting of the problem statement is most essential, for it will be one of the first sections read by a reviewer. If the problem is to eliminate illiteracy in North America, then you'll need billions. If the problem relates to inadequate reading skills for children in a specific elementary school, then $20,000 might be adequate to fund a pilot project. The key point is not stating the problem, per se, but stating a problem that is manageable and solvable.

A problem is a condition that requires some extra effort to fix. It can be a brief statement of an observation. For example, a common problem that is frequently observed is that young, pre-adolescent girls do not achieve as well as expected in science. The problem is not that all girls do not achieve as well as expected. It is a condition focused on a specific group, under a specific context, so we might write a statement such as the following:

> Teachers in our middle school are often unaware that they may be biased against young female students in science classes. As a consequence, girls report being more negatively inclined toward science than are young males. In actual classroom observations, we have found that teachers reward boys more than girls in science classes and that girl-initiated science interactions decline during middle school years. Finally, teacher expectations tend to favor boys. From these observations come two distinct, but related, problems: (1) how can science teachers be made aware of the bias toward girls and (2) what types of training intervention can eliminate sexual bias in middle school science classes?

Reread the statement. Observe how the problem begins with a rather broadly stated issue and then culminates with a very specific, but solvable, problem statement. This is called "V" writing. By giving some general background, the reader, or reviewer in the case of grant proposals, receives enough information to make a smooth transition into a specific condition. You will also observe that the statement is specific and explicit.

In contrast, read the following statement describing a problem:

Home weatherization is not the sole determinant of household energy usage. People's habits can, and do, have serious implications for environmental sustainability. To be effective, conservation education programs must be holistic. Typically, such programs focus on adult consumers with little or no consideration given to the youth who are the future consumers.

Cheap electricity has been one of the key factors that has defined the economic opportunities, environment, and quality of life in the state of. . . . As a result of the increased consumption of electricity, the decade-long surplus of electric energy has disappeared.

To meet this challenge, the state has developed a broad-base energy strategy. An important goal of this strategy is to educate not only the adult consumer, but children as well. As the future consumers of energy, they need to be aware of its monetary and environmental costs. Today it is known that stretching electricity supplies by improving efficiency not only reduces the need for new power plants, but it is also less expensive, less polluting, and avoids the environmental impact of new power plants.

Energy conservation education is a component of the . . . Project. The project includes educational and support groups that enhance the knowledge of home energy conservation, resource allocation, and other pertinent management issues for low-income families. Developing energy literate consumers who will make the right choices regarding their energy needs can only be brought about through conservation education. This, in turn, will contribute to the achievement of the conservation goals. By combining energy education with low-income weatherization and budget management . . . helps its clients to decrease their energy usage and increase both their ability to pay and their personal comfort.

How many times did you have to reread either part or all of that statement? It is confusing. You are not exactly certain what the problem might be or what parts of the problem will be addressed. Needless to say, this proposal was not funded. A problem needs to be written so it is clear and concise. As previously illustrated, the section containing the problem should be carefully prepared so it leads a reviewer from the point of knowing nothing about a specific condition to an informed state. Listed below are a few problem statements that illustrate a straightforward approach.

- Children who attend schools in lower socioeconomic neighborhoods have very limited access to personal computers in their classrooms.
- Volunteers for mathematics tutoring need additional training in the use of math manipulatives.
- The "Reading Recovery Program" is addressing only 40 percent of those needing the service.
- The history program lacks the instructional resources required to meet the criteria of the Bradley Commission.
- Teacher education programs find it increasingly difficult to provide student teachers and interns with ethnic and multicultural experiences.
- Science teaching in grades K-6 focuses on factual or didactic instruction rather than the constructivist model.

These statements illustrate either training or developmental projects. When preparing proposals that are research oriented, you can use other styles. The first example below is stated as a problem. The second is a series of questions. Those are followed by two other examples.

- The major problems associated with clinical blood separation processes for obtaining white blood cells and platelets are low yields, lack of uniformity and purity of yields, and the length of procedures.
- What is the sequence of sensorimotor development leading to complex manipulative abilities? What is the timing of development of manipulative behaviors? What is the role of social context with development of these behaviors?
- During the past six academic years, the school district has experienced a 234 percent increase in reported child abuse cases. The number of cases has increased from 237 to 554. These abused children need extended care to be fully rehabilitated.
- There is not, however, a comprehensive and realistic model describing the dynamic interactions which transfer energy and momentum of wind waves to motions of other frequencies or wave numbers.

Stating the problem is the primary focus of the proposal. All other proposal elements provide support showing how you will address the problem. You may state more than one problem, but if you do, there is a tendency for panel members to conclude that too much is being attempted and they will rank the proposal lower. Perhaps the best advice is to focus on one major problem so panel members know that the proposal is addressing one solvable issue.

Vision Statement

There are a few foundations and agencies that have caught on to that "vision thing" (to quote former President George Bush). Regardless of how you personally feel about the usefulness of vision statements, if a guideline even hints at one, prepare it. A vision statement is not a singular production. You will have to meet with others in your organization to either prepare one or use the official statement that usually appears in handbooks. For example, your institution or school district may be forecasting that the future will have a high-tech focus. Perhaps major capital outlays are being made for computers, laser disk players, multimedia, and peripheral equipment. To show a funder that there is a vision statement, you might create the following:

> **Vision.** Our public schools approach the 21st century with a vision of what education is becoming. A paradigm shift is taking place in learning and teaching requiring the schools to create a supportive environment that combines the best of our cultures and incorporates the unpredictability of the future. Affecting the "new" is the entire realm of technology that now permeates the disciplines of science, mathematics, and engineering. The new educational paradigm creates the expectations that the future requires all students to attain skills that are technologically driven. That drive encompasses the entire spectrum of school learning and adds to it a dimension that provides life skills that are needed in the home, the workplace, and the community at large. Mathematics, science, and technology teachers are key players in applying the basic tenets of the paradigm shift. As educators, we must view the disciplines as being highly interconnected. Several themes and problems require broad-based knowledge to either understand or solve. This does not negate the necessity for specific knowledge bases, but acknowledges how understanding and application of these knowledge bases leads to even greater understanding and a better appreciation for real problem solving.

This vision statement is certainly a noble forecasting of the future and would aid in driving future programs. Other visions may not be so elaborate. A few shorter examples include:

• The vision we have for our classrooms is an environment that stimulates the best achievement that each individual can make, yet stresses the small group cooperation so widely needed in our post-industrial work force.

• Our vision is to prepare administrators who understand the positive interactions of a diverse society and who can enhance the human potential of all who are impacted by our organization.

• The vision guiding this project is that all children can learn. We honor learning and the basic educational and human values associated with the attainment of higher order thinking skills.

• Through successful fruition of this project, we have the opportunity to create a safe and orderly environment in our high school.

Figure 1.1

Evaluation of Problem or Needs Statement

Below is a series of criteria for judging the needs or problem statement. Evaluate each criterion by circling the number to the right of the statement. The higher the score, the better your statement.

NA=Not Applicable
1=Missing
2=Not Readily Apparent
3=Somewhat Apparent
4=Very Apparent

1. Appropriate introduction is provided.		1 2 3 4
2. Logical lead to problem or need statement.		1 2 3 4
3. Problem or need is feasible to address.		1 2 3 4
4. Statistical data support statement.	NA	1 2 3 4
5. If a training project, the "target" group has provided support to the need or problem.	NA	1 2 3 4
6. Assumptions or hypotheses are clearly stated.	NA	1 2 3 4
7. Need or problem appears to be credible.		1 2 3 4
8. Statement is clearly written.		1 2 3 4
9. The statement is presented in a logical order.		1 2 3 4
10. The vision statement is reasonable.	NA	1 2 3 4

11. What is your overall impression of statement?

12. Strengths:

13. Comments for improvement:

Of course, you don't simply put a paragraph of altruistic words down and then do something else. The vision statement is a code that guides present and future behaviors and decisions. In a grant proposal, a vision statement helps to establish the tone of why a specific set of objectives and activities are being suggested. If the guidelines do not request the inclusion of a vision statement, then you must ask yourself, "Does the vision statement add or detract from the proposal?" Figure 1.1 can be used to judge your first statements of the need or problem.

Priorities

A priority is a statement about the importance or merit of selected issues, actions, or circumstances. Often you will read a statement listing the priorities of certain courses of action. In some cases, you may have a list of six or seven attributes or conditions. The trick in listing priorities is to realize that they have an order about them. To state that "these seven priorities are equal" implies that you do not have a list of priorities at all. Priorities have a rank-ordering character about them and you need to address the top priority first, the secondary one next, and so on. It is important as you seek systematic funding that the emphasis goes to the top priority.

Establish Priorities for Funding

Grant proposal writers may be classified into one of two groups—*opportunists* and *problem solvers*. Opportunists have the motto, "If there's a dollar out there, let's go for it." These are the individuals who dash off proposals with little crafting or careful designing. They are the ones who see a chance to get a grant and proceed with little regard as to how the money will impact their organization. If somebody is funding at-risk programs, then crank out something on the at-risk. If there is money for writing across the curriculum, then get some. You see the point? The problem with adopting an opportunistic view of proposal writing is that even when funded, the infrastructure is not going to accept the program once the grant is exhausted.

Opportunists tend to act without working with those who must implement the project. The history of Title III of the Elementary and Secondary Education Act is replete with unsuccessfully implemented projects. Yes, I realize how tempting it is to a principal or curriculum director to target a fast buck. But the overall impact of opportunism is to expend organizational energy on counterproductive, time-consuming projects that have no payoff for the future.

The opposite position is that of problem solvers. This perspective treats developing grant proposals as an integral part of funding activities that help an organization meet the priorities that have been established. More importantly, the process is democratic and open. Everyone is explicitly invited to participate in the design of meaningful projects. Typically, in organizations that adopt the opportunistic modus operandi, a small clique writes only for itself. By having open and public work sessions, problem solvers allow the creative juices to flow and a healthy interaction of ideas to take place. Problems are not solved by authoritarian dictums. It is vitally important for all individuals in the institution or organization to openly discuss the perspective to which they subscribe. Such policy discussions help to establish a vision of why outside funding is solicited. Clearly, it distinguishes "good" money from "bad," as there are always numerous funders who support just about every conceivable project. Time is short in all organizations. Thus, it behooves administrators and nonadministrators alike to have a priority listing of what needs urgent, outside funding. Such a list helps channel the time-consuming efforts of proposal writing to the most constructive and worthwhile uses.

The Priorities of Funders

The biggest mistake any grant proposal writer can make is to assume that once they have a carefully crafted document, it is ready for submission. No, not yet. At this point I suggest identifying funding sources with priorities that coincide with yours. Every funding agency has either explicitly written funding priorities or implicitly stated ones. Before you begin the work of preparing proposals for your number one priority, examine the various reports, directories, and guidelines of funders. Chapter 2 presents a rather detailed strategy on how to monitor funding sources, so at this point I will be general rather than specific. Once you have a funder's report or guidelines, carefully examine its current funding priorities. If you observe that a certain business only funds proposals from Marin County, California, then do not read any further if your organization is located out of Marin County. Many foundations are geographically bound; they only fund proposals that emanate from a specified geographic sector. Funders will specify if they provide money for scholarships, basic research, capital improvements, remodeling, equipment, or travel. Pay careful attention to these explicitly stated priorities.

What should you do if you examine a guideline and it is silent about priorities? This requires some probing in one of the sources listed in Appendix A. Examine what types of projects were funded last year or in the immediate past. If you note that they did not fund any local school districts, then it is safe to conclude that they do not. Often grant seekers assume that if a funder has never funded "my type" of proposal, then "I'll be their first to be funded." Wrong— you will not be the first because it is obvious from their previous funding patterns that your type of proposal is not being funded. The final action might be a telephone call to the agency office with a specific query not discussed in the various reports. They will quickly tell you if they fund in that arena. The essence of this discussion is that you play the probabilities of being funded. You have a higher probability of being funded if like types of projects have been previously funded. This line of reasoning can change if a new funding priority is established. That is one reason for carefully monitoring funding sources in a systematic manner. In Chapter 2 we will discuss in detail how to organize your group to become more successful in finding those funding agencies interested in your priorities.

The basic thread of this chapter has been on how to think about crafting the grant proposal. Our orientation, for the most part, has been on writing rather small dollar amount projects. Let us now shift our orientation to the means that are necessary to design really big projects.

Writing Big Proposals

Successful proposals for external support of institutional needs may be generated in a variety of ways. This section describes one model that may be useful when developing comprehensive improvement proposals involving several disciplines or units. Many of the suggestions may not be applicable in preparing smaller, more focused proposals involving one writer. These tips are applicable, however, when you need to work with even one other colleague who resides in a different unit. Several important steps in proposal development should take place before the project plan is actually written. Careful attention to the preliminary aspects results in a better proposal and improves chances for funding.

Insufficient resources for meeting institutional goals and objectives often force faculty and other institutional officials to seek external support for their programs. Prior to seeking such support, a necessary step is to ask faculty and administrators to identify and prioritize significant needs among those existing at the institution. It is essential to decide whether a comprehensive improvement plan or one focusing on a narrowly defined area can best address those needs. In searching for sources of external support, funding agency goals and objectives should be compared with those of the institution's improvement goals. A reasonable match between the two must be reflected before developing a proposal. Program guidelines should be thoroughly examined for information relating to eligibility and limitations; matching requirements, if any; and proposal deadlines.

Expanding the Circle

After an agency or foundation program is identified as one for which a proposal might be developed, it is important to enlarge the circle of people at the institution, both faculty and administrators, who will be involved in developing the proposal. Early involvement is necessary to determine the extent of receptivity of colleagues and administrators to the proposed plan and to gauge the specific assistance that can be expected from them. Forms of assistance might include data collection, budget and proposal preparation, review of the final proposal, and identification of specific roles for faculty in the plan. Discussions with faculty members can reveal who is interested in becoming involved in the project, in what ways, to what extent, and what relevant skills they can bring to the project.

At this point at least three local administrative procedures must be met: determine whose approval is needed (president, dean, division/department chairperson, curriculum committee); how much time may be required in the approval chain; and who can provide various pieces of information (e.g., indirect cost rate, enrollment data). In the public schools, it would be superintendent, principal, curriculum director, and faculty.

Now is the time to determine whether similar proposals have been submitted by the institution in the recent past as well as their final outcome. If appropriate, verbatim reviewer comments should be requested and examined to learn the reasons why previous proposals were not successful. It is also possible to request copies of successful proposals submitted to federal agency programs by other institutions of comparable size, type, and location with similar needs and problems. These can provide useful information about ideas being tried elsewhere, methods of data collection, and proposal styles.

Four other important questions need to be considered at this stage. Have previous projects related to the one under consideration been funded at the institution? If so, is there potential duplication or overlap between them? Are others in the institution now developing improvement proposals? Is there possible duplication or overlap?

If other agencies or groups are to be involved in the project, they must be included from the start. More than likely, compromises will be necessary relating to the scope or magnitude of the proposal. Most organizations, such as school districts, need the official endorsement of their board of trustees. They usually meet once a month. Their support requires very careful and detailed long-range planning. Further, if there is need for some type of interagency committee, that group needs to be identified and formally invited to participate.

Preparing the Concept Paper

The next major step is developing an outline of problems and the proposed plan to solve them. Continued dialogue and "brainstorming" with others are vital at this stage. Alternative solutions to problems should be considered. Carefully develop the rationale for the final solutions you're seeking to have funded. Locally available resources that might be obtained without outside funding need to be identified. A literature search may be appropriate to see if others have already done work in areas included in the preliminary plans (e.g., developing instructional modules, preparing multimedia systems, or computer courseware).

Preliminary costs, time estimates for project implementation, and roles for key project personnel need to be detailed at this point. Guidelines of the program to which the proposal will be submitted should be rechecked to be certain that there is a proper match. Another search for alternative or additional funding sources might also be appropriate at this point.

Supporting data, and descriptions of existing programs and facilities to validate the institution's request for assistance, are crucial in proposal development and to those to whom the proposal will be submitted. It is important to present clear and accurate baseline data in the proposed improvement plan. Some of the items that probably should be included are: total institutional enrollment, enrollment in relevant courses, number of specific majors, and any significant changes in recent years in each of these; a description of fields in which majors are offered and other course offerings; physical facilities, including major equipment holdings; student retention rates; student performance on standardized tests, as appropriate; number of graduates pursuing advanced degrees—disciplines, institutions; and profiles of the faculty, including total number, number in respective disciplines, types of degrees held, minority representation, and specific skills that are relevant to the proposed project. Other information needed before writing the final proposal and budget include: up-to-date descriptions and costs of equipment and materials proposed for purchase; travel costs; identification of consultants; and institutional rates for staff benefits, staff replacements, consultants, and indirect costs. If the institution does not have an established indirect cost rate, the business office will need to contact the agency's grants and contracts office regarding the establishment of such a rate. This step would lead to submitting organization, management, and financial information to qualify for indirect cost recovery. (The concept of indirect costs is discussed in Chapter 6.)

While specific proposals may require other additional preliminary activities because of special features, for the most part, you should be ready to draft a complete proposal setting forth what your institution wants to do, why and how it is to be done, who will be involved and in what ways, how success will be measured, and how successful outcomes of the project will be "institutionalized."

Finalizing the Proposal

There are two additional important steps to be considered before developing the final version of the proposal. Discussions should be held with appropriate institutional officials regarding any and all implied institutional obligations during the project as well as after the project ceases. Their explicit endorsement and support in the final proposal are critical. In some funding programs it will be necessary, as part of the proposal, to include a signed "Local Review Statement" showing formal endorsement by an appropriate institutional official. Many foundations will only accept one proposal from an institution, so be certain that yours is that one. Further, there may be need for an institutional review board statement, especially if human subjects are involved. In addition, the draft proposal should be reviewed by others with key roles in the project for their concurrence on the final project plan.

Prior to submitting the proposal, it is also advisable to ask two or more colleagues not involved in developing the proposal to review it, applying the criteria published in the agency's guidelines. When the proposal is submitted to peer review by the funding program, reviewers will use these same criteria. (Remember, reviewers will judge the merit of the proposal based only on what is presented in it.)

After suggestions resulting from the colleague review have been carefully considered, the final proposal should be prepared and submitted to the agency in sufficient time to meet any established closing date.

A list of key points follows. These will be useful as a proposal is developed. The list could be used as a final checklist to make sure that there are no major omissions from the proposal. Of course, one must always remember: Follow the published guidelines.

Checklist for Proposal Development

Responsibility—Recognize that as proposed project director, you are accepting a responsibility on behalf of your colleagues, your institution, and, ultimately, your students.

Institutional Needs—Identify and prioritize pressing unmet institutional needs. Make sure your institution's goals and proposal objectives are compatible with those of the funding source. Don't chase dollars for dollar's sake.

Institutional and Staff Capability—Be certain that what is being proposed is something your institution can do well and that the staff available on campus can carry out the effort.

Planning—Involve other faculty; get approval and support of the central administration and outside agencies if needed.

Chain of Reasoning—Repeat or maintain central ideas throughout the proposal.

Data Collection—Do it early in the proposal development process; present it clearly; make sure information is up-to-date and accurate.

Positive Writing Style—Avoid using maybe, probably, hopefully, and might.

Jargon—Avoid it!

Scope of Effort—Make sure it is reasonable, feasible, and economical.

Timetable—Make it realistic; list major project milestones.

Budget—Be certain that items in the budget are discussed and justified in the narrative and that items or positions discussed in the narrative are reflected in the budget.

Key Project Personnel—Briefly describe their responsibilities and skills relevant to the project. Append vitae.

Outreach—Give evidence that ideas will be useful to others and that they are transferable.

Expected Outcomes—Describe what could result from the proposed effort if all goes well.

Monitoring/Evaluation—Show how you plan to find out if the project is accomplishing what was intended. Describe specific plans for measuring project impact.

Continuation Plans—Give specific evidence of your institution's commitment to continue successful components of the proposed projet.

Colleague Review—Have colleagues review the proposal prior to submission using criteria published in the guidelines.

Clearinghouse Approval—Obtain a state clearinghouse number if one is required.

Endorsements—Append letters of endorsements from agencies or affiliated groups to show their support.

Assurances—Complete institutional review board assurances as needed.

Mechanics—Number pages, proofread, have proper signatures, assemble correctly, and follow organizational instructions in the guidelines.

Deadlines—Send proposal via certified, receipt return mail at least five days prior to the announced deadline date, or send by guaranteed parcel delivery service at least two days in advance of the deadline.

2
Monitoring Funding Sources

No QUESTION ABOUT IT, THERE IS ALWAYS A SENSE OF VICTORY WHEN you receive the long-awaited letter from the granting agency and it begins, "We are pleased. . . ." No need to read any farther; that lead is only sent when you receive a grant award. Individuals are often funded on a routine basis without carefully monitoring the various sources used by professional grant seekers. When this happens, it is a case of luck and opportunity converging. However, if a school, a school district, a nonprofit agency, or an institution of higher education wants to maximize its grant writing efforts, then some type of organizational commitment must be made.

Organizing an Infrastructure to Locate Funding Sources____

Assuming your organization has democratically identified its funding priorities and everyone knows the type of projects that will be encouraged or supported, a need exists for some type of office or appointed individual who is the designated grant seeker. This person is responsible for monitoring various guides and resource indexes and informing all others of the news. In short, if an institution or school district truly wants to be efficient, it must establish an Office of Grant Development. Major universities, that is, those ranked in the top 100 in research or extramural funds, all have some type of helping group to inform the faculty of potential opportunities.

The key to success in such an operation is to select a person who is a supporter of ideas, not a blocker of them.

The individual who heads such an effort must be one who wants to work with others and is truly a reflective leader. These individuals bask in the successes that others have in writing funded grant proposals. I am making an extended point here because there are known school districts with grants managers who are threatened by any faculty feedback or suggestions for possible proposals.

Establishing the Office

If the office is centralized in a school district or institution of higher education (IHE), then the central office must make a conscious effort to alert everyone of funding potentials. How is this instigated? The first task is to monitor relevant federal, state, foundation, and business guides. In Appendix A there is a detailed list of selected key guides. Once the search is complete, some type of newsletter should be distributed so that news and deadlines are received in a timely fashion.

A file listing the interests of all staff members should also be established. The data can be collected and easily converted to computer databases so that as new items are discovered, the right people are promptly notified. Realize that not everyone will want to know about every funding source.

A third major task for the office is to assemble writing teams. Most proposals will have more than one person involved, and writing teams help forge commitment to implementation. A fourth task is to conduct inservice training on proposal writing; another is to act as the central clearinghouse to expedite the processing and submitting of the required proposals.

An Office in One School

It may also be feasible to establish a decentralized proposal development office. Virtually no school can assign a full-time person to monitor grant potentials and conduct the five major tasks outlined above. This means that the building administrator or departmental chair, in the case of IHE's, must provide someone with released time to help monitor funding sources and help colleagues prepare proposals.

Whatever the model used, it is clear that to maximize your chances for long-term success, there needs to be some formal organization, office, or mechanism in place. Establishing such an office is investing in the organization and its future.

Seeking Governmental Sources

The number of federal government agencies awarding grants to schools, businesses, foundations, nonprofit groups, universities, and other pubic agencies is staggering—about 1,350 programs and 51 agencies. The Feds disseminate news about funding opportunities through three very different sources.

Catalog of Federal Domestic Assistance

The most important index for identifying federal resources is the *Catalog of Federal Domestic Assistance* (CFDA). The CFDA is an absolute must for anyone seeking federal assistance, be it funds, equipment, or services. This loose-leaf, five-inch thick compendium is published each year by the General Services Administration under the Office of Management and Budget. At least once each year, a supplement is provided so that the programs are kept current.

The CFDA contains nearly everything. It is divided into three basic sections: (1) indexes, (2) program descriptions, and (3) appendixes. As you open the cover, there are six easy-to-use indexes. The first is the Agency Index Summary describing the functions and activities of the respective federal agencies responsible for administering programs. A five-digit CFDA number is assigned to every program. These numbers are always the same for each department or agency. Figure 2.1 contains a selected listing of the CFDA two-digit prefixes. Once you know that NASA is 43 or Education is 84, those are the only numbers you need, and you can locate specific programs by the last three digits of a five-digit number (e.g., 84.164).

The second index is the Agency Program Index that lists, in numerical order by five-digits, all programs, titles, agency responsible, and the kind of assistance being offered—financial, nonfinancial, or combined.

Figure 2.1

Some Basic Two-Digit Prefixes Used in the *Catalog of Federal Domestic Assistance*

CFDA Prefix Number	Selected U.S. Department or Agency
10	Agriculture
11	Commerce
12	Defense
14	Housing and Urban Development
15	Interior
16	Justice
17	Labor
19	State
20	Transportation
21	Treasury
39	General Services Administration
42	Library of Congress
43	National Aeronautics and Space Administration
45	National Endowment for the Arts and Humanities
59	Small Business Administration
64	Veterans Affairs
66	Environmental Protection Agency
68	National Gallery of Art
81	Energy
82	Information Agency
84	Education
85	Harry S. Truman Scholarship Foundation
89	National Archives and Records Administration
93	Health and Human Services

Source: *Catalog of Federal Domestic Assistance.* (1995). The Office of Management and Budget: Washington, D.C.

The Functional Index Summary lists categories of support (e.g., "Resource Conservation and Development"). Listed under that title are five different agencies and a total of 26 different programs identified by that five-digit CFDA number. Under the category of "Higher Education and Training," 39 different programs are listed by title.

There is also a Subject Index providing a detailed listing of programs by various topics. Included here are popular names, services, or selected beneficiaries all followed by that five-digit number. For example, under "Computers" are 18 topics and 26 different CFDA numbers. No question about it, the index system is designed to be user friendly.

The second main section is the compilation of Program Descriptions arranged in numerical order from 10.001, Agricultural Research—Basic and Applied, to CFDA number 93.995 (1,082 pages later), Adolescent Family Life—Demonstration Projects. These components of the CFDA provide a major piece for a grant seeker's toolbox. Each program is described with 16 items of information.

1. Agency
2. Authorization
3. Objectives
4. Types of Assistance
5. Uses and Restrictions
6. Eligibility Requirements
7. Application and Award Process
8. Assistance Considerations
9. Post-Assistance Requirements
10. Financial Information
11. Program Accomplishments
12. Regulations, Guidelines, and Literature
13. Information Contacts
14. Related Programs
15. Examples of Funded Projects
16. Criteria for Selecting Proposals

Having all that information before you gives you an advantage over all others who are not aware of the CFDA. For example, the description lists the program's appropriation along with the range of previous awards and an average award. Knowing these figures, you can better gauge the scope of your intended project.

Further, if you have any questions about the program, a contact person is listed. I always telephone this person and ask the size of the competition as well as how many awards will be funded, how many are new, and how many are renewals. You see, I play the probabilities. If there are only three awards nationally and the program officer expects 300 applications, the odds of being funded are 1 in 100 or a 1 percent probability. I will not enter that one. It is just too risky. If you run fourth, you get—as they say in the rodeo business—only the applause.

The CFDA has much more, including a deadlines index and several informational appendixes. I love the CFDA as a federal toolbox. You simply need to spend an hour with it. (But not curled-up in your lap, it's too big for that—maybe propped open on an old door.)

The Federal Register

Ever heard the term "red tape"? Well, the *Federal Register* (FR) is the red tape. Every weekday, the FR is published by the U.S. Government Printing Office. It is a necessary item for your grant seeker toolbox since it provides the rules and regulations that guide all those 1,350 federal programs. Since you never know when programs will be announced, you need the FR. Basically, the FR provides the following and much more:

Presidential Orders
Program Rules and Regulations
Proposed Rules
Notices of Advisory Meetings
Program Announcements
Requests for Application
Deadline Dates

For our purposes, we want to know the deadline dates for various programs. The Department of Education often publishes several dozen deadline dates in various issues of the FR. These deadlines are often more current than those found in the CFDA, and each program is identified by the five-digit CFDA number. These two documents need to be used in tandem. The CFDA gives all the program details. The FR gives additional information, new deadlines, rules and regulations affecting the program, funding information, and a program officer or contact person with a telephone number.

Often new programs are first announced by proposed rules and regulations. The proposed "rules and regs" change very little from the final ones, so get your teams organized and start writing. This gives you a great time advantage over the uninformed competition. Contact the identified program officer and ask for the application materials. If new ones are not yet ready, request a copy of last year's. Be proactive; that's why you systematically monitor the CFDA and FR.

When proposed rules and regs are printed, you are invited to respond. Send the noted official your candid comments. You just may help shape the direction of the red tape. When notices of advisory meetings are given, and it is a program that meets your priorities, call and ask for a summary of the meeting—not the minutes. The minutes are not published until approved at a subsequent meeting. By having a summary, you know what direction the program may take. It is all part of being proactive.

There is much more in the FR, for example, the index to the *Code of Federal Regulations* (CFR). This set of documents contains the codified general and permanent rules that are published in the *Federal Register*. There are 50 different CFR titles. Education's code is 34. These items are really useful to your business office.

Commerce Business Daily

The last major resource used to identify federal sources is the *Commerce Business Daily* (CBD). As the name implies, this document is published each working day like the FR. The average person may not ever use the CBD, but if you are seeking to participate fully by providing goods or services to the federal government, then this is a necessity.

The federal government does not really own many businesses other than the U.S. mint and the armed forces. Virtually all governmental services are bid out to the private sector for a tidy $200 billion per year. These services range from scrubbing the halls of a local post office to building the B-1 bomber. Surprised? Most people are. To take part in the bidding process, subscribe to the CBD. It lists all the desired government procurements, services, supplies, property sales, training, leasing, repair, and expert or consultant services.

There are actually 97 codes used in the CBD by which services and supplies are classified. Nineteen different letter codes describe the types of services being requested. A few are listed here:

A   Experimental, Development, Test, Research
H   Expert and Consultant Service
U   Training Service
Y   Construction

There are 78 two-digit codes for supplies, equipment, and materials:

14   Guided Missiles
48   Valves
69   Training Aids and Devices
76   Books, Maps, and Other Publications

By reviewing the respective alphabet codes, which can be purchased separately, you'll find what the federal government wants in each issue. Next, contact the person listed for a Request for Proposal (RFP). By mail or electronically you will receive a printed description of what the government requires and how offers will be evaluated. Send in your bid, carefully following the conditions set in the RFP. Typically, the top contenders are requested to renegotiate the contract. Finally, an award is given based on a combination of the lowest price and technical merit of the bidders. The CBD also lists the winners of awards in each issue. As mentioned earlier, most schools do not compete in this arena. It is really for the professionals.

Foundation Resources

In the United States there is one federal government, 50 state governments, and 37,571 different foundations. You don't have to use modern math to realize that the private sector plays a major role in public philanthropy. It is rather easy to apply for funding, but you really have to do a good deal of homework before you dash off that letter seeking foundation support. Actually, the strategies suggested in searching federal grants are almost identical when seeking potential foundation donors.

Recall your first step in seeking government sources was the *Catalog of Federal Domestic Assistance* (CFDA). Similar resources are available for examining foundation funding priorities. A good fast start here is *The Foundation 1,000*. This 2,826-page tome provides a detailed listing of the

1,000 largest foundations in the United States. These large foundations contribute almost two-thirds of the yearly donations made. How do you use this resource?

Check the index. An excellent index is included so that your specific subject area can be identified. Once you find a potential funder, study the pattern of gifts that have been made. In most cases, the profiles will show current funding priorities, geographic or spending limitations, key foundation officers, assets, and descriptions of recently funded groups. You need to examine all the information given in the profile so that you select exactly the right foundation.

As you examine previous gifts, look for those with similar purposes to what you are pursuing. For example, you might want scholarship support for deserving students. If you notice that no scholarship support is listed in the profile, act no further. Do not delude yourself that you can make such a grand case that your organization will be the first. Funding patterns are changed by foundations only when they modify their announced funding priorities. In cases where the founder of the trust has specified rigid limitations, the priorities may not be changed.

The 28th edition of the *Annual Register of Grant Support: A Directory of Funding Sources* provides a comprehensive list of 3,155 North American grant-making groups. Included are foundations, businesses, unions, governmental agencies, professional associations, and others. Rather detailed summaries are provided about each entry. After examining the index and studying the summary, you can make a decision whether to initiate contact with potential funders. This 1,251-page directory will be a checkpoint against other directories as you follow a specific foundation. *The Foundation Directory*, 17th edition, lists 7,293 entries and is limited to those foundations making awards of at least $200,000 yearly and having $2 million in assets. This source is helpful in cross-checking a foundation to be certain that it makes large enough contributions. Finally, there is the *Guide to U.S. Foundations, Their Trustees, Officers, and Donors*. This guide has 37,211 entries, 3,054 pages, and includes 33,983 foundations. It has a compilation of all state and local foundation directories. Knowing how to access all the foundations in your state can be most helpful as you develop a long-range funding plan. In addition to these four resources, Appendix A provides an annotated listing of several other excellent source books presenting foundation profiles available to grant seekers.

Contacting Foundations

One awkward experience I had was watching a grant seeker and his secretary stuffing a few hundred envelopes with a duplicated letter. I asked what they were doing and they answered, "Writing to a bunch of foundations and businesses to get a grant." Let me caution you, this is *not* the way to approach businesses or foundations. Form letters are discarded without reply. Instead, carefully match your funding needs with the funding priorities of the foundation.

Once you narrow the list to those having the highest probabilities of funding your proposal, write a letter of inquiry. Introduce your organization, explain your goal and how it fits the apparent priorities of the foundation, mention your IRS 501(c)(3) nonprofit designation, and that you would like to submit a full proposal. All of this is done on one page. The reason for brevity is that the vast bulk of foundations do not have paid staff to process correspondence. Most have only one person at the office. Thousands have no one. If you cannot state your query in one page, it probably won't be read.

I mentioned the IRS 501(c)(3) nonprofit designation. The Federal Internal Revenue Service officially designates the nonprofit organizations in the United States. In order for you to receive any foundation money, your group must be legally described as a nonprofit organization. The very least is that it be declared a state nonprofit organization. The secretary of state at your state capital can send you the necessary forms to incorporate as a nonprofit group. This is usually the first step to gaining an IRS designation. The IRS forms are more detailed than those of the state. Even school districts and institutions of higher education should seek the federal, nonprofit designation. Thousands of grant-making foundations require it because it is important for them to maintain their tax-exempt foundation status.

The emphasis above is on a group or an organization. The reason for the explicitness is that foundations rarely fund individuals. Sure, the John D. and Catherine T. MacArthur Foundation has made the day for scores of people who were judged as being among the nation's most talented or creative individuals. But in the main, foundations fund organizations. This obviously precludes scholarships, travel grants, or honors.

Once you contact a person at the foundation and obtain either their funding priorities or their guidelines, the rest is up to you. For the most part, foundations use a two-phase application process. In phase one, they suggest sending a short summary or abstract of the proposed project. Typically, this one- or two-page piece contains: (1) a need or problem and significance, (2) goals and objectives, (3) procedures or methodology, (4) an evaluation model, (5) personnel, (6) a short budget note, and (7) an IRS 501(c)(3) letter. These components will be thoroughly discussed later. The acceptance rate of the initial phase applications is usually low. In some cases, they are declined at a rate of 98 percent or more.

Assuming invitation to phase two, you will be asked to submit a full proposal. A page limitation is generally given, usually about 15 pages total. The phase two application amplifies the six key points noted above. At stage two, you have rather favorable odds of being funded—from 50 to 100 percent. A similar two-phase approach is used by several federal agencies including The National Science Foundation (NSF) and the Fund for the Improvement of Post-Secondary Education (FIPSE).

As I implied earlier, most of those 37,000 plus foundations are mom-and-pop organizations. That term is not used pejoratively, but to describe their modus operandi. If you can contact the founders or benefactors personally, so much the better. Foundation funders like to know who they are supporting. Funding decisions have been known to be made from the heart.

In some cases, you may have a project that is too large for smaller foundations and yet not in the funding priority of larger ones. In this case, you subdivide the project by some logical means and contact different foundations with one aspect of the full project. Inform each how you are subdividing the project and who is being contacted for what. Honesty is an absolute in this business.

One question that is frequently asked of me is, "May I submit the same proposal to different foundations?" The answer is always, "No!" It is not ethical to submit simultaneous applications, and the funders often compare notes on formal or informal bases. Once the people involved in philanthropy realize that you are simply mooching, your reputation will precede you.

Again, successful foundation grant seekers spend hours examining annual reports, statements, and even the IRS 990-PF forms to determine the best probability for funding. The IRS 990-PF forms are submitted each year by all foundations. Every grant that is awarded is listed in this handy form. You can obtain a copy of any foundation's fiscal report by contacting a field office of the Internal Revenue Service or by contacting any public library that has been designated a funding center. The Foundation Center of New York City designates selected libraries in the United States as Foundation Center Libraries and each local center has a wealth of bibliographic information, plus most of the reference books that you'll ever need to identify a potential funder. The sites are listed in *The Foundation Directory*. These sources are important since only 800 foundations publish any form of public annual report.

Contacting the Business Sector

Writing a letter requesting assistance from some large corporation or business is tempting, but they tend to link philanthropy with public relations. The little truism "businesses tend to fund in the shadow of their smokestacks" sums up business funding. If Hewlett-Packard has a major plant in your town or county, you might contact them, otherwise, your time will be wasted.

Typically, to seek assistance from a large corporation, you initiate contact with the firm's public relations office. If they have a separate philanthropic office, it will be conveyed through public relations. Businesses operate very similarly to foundations. Most require a two-phase application. There are more than 1,900 businesses and corporations that fund a company foundation. For example, the Weyerhauser Company funds its own Weyerhauser Company Foundation; The International Paper Company, likewise. The key to corporate giving is their annual profit and loss statement. If business is brisk and profits are growing, then corporate funding to their respective foundations or public relations offices increases. Before you write that carefully crafted letter to the Exxon Corporation, check its most recent annual report. If profits are up, send the request. If profits are down, you might seek elsewhere.

As with foundations, businesses and corporations like to know the recipients of their generosity. Any potential meeting of the "right person" in the corporate structure is helpful. Many companies have a formal application process. Others tend to be more informal. For the latter, use the generic model being described in this book.

One last point: Funders usually meet once, twice, or four times each year to evaluate grant proposals. It is important to find out what months the group meets. In that manner, you can time the arrival of your letter or full proposal to arrive for the pending meeting. If you miss one deadline, you must wait until the next to find out how you fared. Please do not telephone the company to ask about the status of your proposal. They will notify you.

A key resource for identifying potential private sector funders is the *National Directory of Corporate Giving: A Guide to Corporate Giving Programs and Corporate Funding*. More than 2,000 companies are cataloged and their programs of interest listed. In addition, by subscribing to one of the various weekly grant services such as *Education Grants Alert*, you will receive numerous tips about corporate funding sources.

Contacting foundations and businesses is an art. Keep in mind that the emphasis in this book is grant proposal writing. It is not fund-raising. Fund-raising is an entirely different field that we will delimit. Remember, the funders have all been successful in some line of work. They did not become financially successful by taking unnecessary risks. As you craft your letter or proposal, work in the message that what you are suggesting is a practical and successful idea. Few, if any, businesses, corporations, or foundations will fund some risky sounding adventure. There are some questions to be asked about all potential funders to help you make the best match. Below is a detailed checklist of questions that you need to know about your potential funder.

A Checklist of Questions for Knowing the Funder

1. Does the funder allocate funds on some established priority?

2. How many dollars does the funder have available to award for project activity this year? How does this figure compare to the figure for previous years, including last year?

3. What is the average size of a grant or contract that has been authorized for the prior year of the funder? Can you obtain a list of these awards, including project title, principal investigator, and address? Is there a maximum amount that can be awarded to any one recipient?

4. Does the funder consider itself in the seed-money area of project support, or does it make it a policy to continue with project support if promising results are obtained? If so, how much of the current year's funds are earmarked for the continuation of existing projects and how much is to help initiate new projects?

5. Does the funder conduct a preliminary screening of proposal concepts based on a letter of intent to submit before actually giving the go-ahead to submit a full proposal?

6. Does the funder have guidelines prepared for use by organizations in preparing proposals? If not, does the funder have a set of regulations that are used internally in the administration of project grants? If not, and the funder is a state or federal agency, can they supply you with a copy of specific legislation under which the funding program is authorized?

7. Does the funder seek to allocate or award project funds on the basis of geographic location of the recipients?

8. What restrictions apply to project funds?

9. Are projects budgeted so that the awarded funds cover all of the direct costs of doing projects? Are you required to put up some percentage of matching funds at the local level? If so, can the matching amount be in kind costs on the part of your own organization or must they be in cash?

10. In the case of projects that involve developing a product (e.g., an instrument, a book, a computer program, a set of instructional materials), who retains the rights to the material? Who can copyright the material?

11. Does the funder have a deadline for the receipt of applications or proposals for funding?

12. Can you obtain a copy of a previously successful proposal or contract that has been funded?

3
Establishing Needs

A SIGNIFICANT NUMBER OF FUNDED PROJECTS RELATE TO STAFF
development, program development, or offering a service. A
successful proposal for funding these activities or others
will generally include a "need statement" or objective data
that demonstrate the need. These data are gathered by
conducting a needs assessment.

Preparing a successful needs assessment combines the
art of sensing what requires improvement with the science
of collecting accurate data for basing predictions. Thus,
needs assessments depend on planning, determining what
data to collect, and providing decision makers with
coherent statements about well identified areas requiring
new or continued fiscal or material support. It is also
important to identify the human resources already in the
organization. Untapped human resources should be
marshaled to remedy identified problems or needs. State
and federal grant proposals require a needs assessment to
justify funding, so you must learn to prepare them
effectively and persuasively. The tips described in this
chapter are tested techniques that can be adapted to any
specific grant proposal.

Conducting Needs Assessments

Many methods are available to assess needs. Below are a
few selected techniques:

> Testimonials from knowledgeable individuals
> Statements from professional or scientific societies
> Committee reports
> Planning documents
> Reviews of literature

While these techniques are far from all-inclusive and somewhat self-explanatory, this chapter will highlight the following:

Scores on objective or standardized tests
Surveys
Discrepancy models
Delphi technique
Focus groups

These general methods are highlighted because they tend to be used most easily and more widely by school districts and universities and are most economical to conduct and interpret.

A need may be defined as a condition that requires attention, or some desire or value that is not present or not being met. In many cases, needs are simply what someone or some group wants. Educational needs tend to arise from changing conditions or circumstances, and they are identified as needs relatively late in the process.

Identifying needs is essential in planning for and involving the community in educational goal setting. A needs assessment is a method of discovering gaps between *what is* and *what ought* to take place in schools. The difference between reality and desire is frequently referred to as a discrepancy.

Needs assessments are conducted to:

• Discover strengths of programs or personnel.
• Identify perceived weaknesses in programs or personnel.
• Determine discrepancies in programs or curriculums.
• Identify unmet concerns.
• Assist curriculum development through evaluation.
• Set priorities for future or immediate actions.
• Illustrate a novel local want.
• Justify renewal of special programs.
• Provide for community consensus.
• Share the general decision making among various constituencies.

When conducting a needs assessment, you must determine what client group will receive the intended service and if there will be intermediate groups also participating. The responses from these individuals and their respective groups will then be summarized and included in your data set.

Achievement Tests

One good use for those often used, but ignored, standardized tests is to establish a need in some specific area. Achievement tests assess a student's terminal behavior or the expected attainment of the student after completing an assignment, unit, module, or course. Such test scores tend to illustrate levels of skills development. Use the data from any state or nationally normed test with great caution. The first question to ask is, "Did we teach the domain of that content before the test was taken?" If not, any poor showings on the subscales of the test can be ignored. If major concepts have been taught and the students still did poorly, examine the quality of instruction (the teacher) and the quality of the curriculum. To improve achievement-test scores requires detailed analyses of scores on a school-by-school basis. Further, the fastest possible gain on normed tests is usually two years.

Assuming valid tests, the data should be interpreted by the grant proposal writing group for specific trends. Remember, a need is not "to improve mathematics proficiency." That is too global. You improve specific skills, processes, and competencies. To identify these requires disaggregating the data into component sectors, schools, grades, and gender. Such an analysis will point to a specific need and will show the importance of maximizing student achievement through specific, data-based interventions.

Surveys

The typical needs assessment is usually a short questionnaire distributed to all appropriate personnel in the organization. It may contain open-ended and forced-response items. If surveys are used, multiple sets of needs questionnaires must be administered to subgroups. This method is like a marketing approach for determining concerns and providing successful solutions. Before employing this technique, it is important that decision makers carefully examine the advantages and disadvantages of forced-response questionnaires for determining needs.

The following list summarizes the general advantages of using a questionnaire to collect needs data:

- Many individuals can be contacted at the same time, usually through the school district's mail service.
- A questionnaire is less expensive to administer than a personal interview.
- Each selected subgroup respondent receives identical questions.
- A written questionnaire provides a vehicle for expression without fear of embarrassment to the respondent.
- Responses are easily tabulated, depending on the design of the instrument.
- Uniform data are gathered that allow for long-range research implications and for program development.

Disadvantages to this approach:

- The investigator is prevented from learning the respondent's motivation for answering questions.
- Respondents may be somewhat limited in providing free expression of opinions, owing to instrument design.
- Not all questionnaires are returned.
- Complex designs cause poor responses, or no response at all.
- A question may have different meanings to different people.
- Selections of the sample, per se, may cause biased results; that is, the sample may not be representative of the population.
- Respondents may not complete the entire questionnaire.

The timing of a survey is critical and must also be considered. September, December, January, May, and June are very poor months to distribute questionnaires. July and August are totally inappropriate for mailing questionnaires to school personnel because they are on vacation. And, in addition to seasonal constraints, many school districts have policies specifying that no one in the district is obliged to complete a questionnaire not officially approved by the district.

Open-Ended Questions. An open-ended question typically does not include predetermined or forced-response categories, and the respondent is free to answer in any manner desired. There are at least five reasons for asking an open-ended question: (1) to probe an idea further, (2) to accommodate categories that are incomplete or inadequate in a forced-response list, (3) to provide projective situations, (4) to generate items for forced-response surveys, and (5) to elicit items for a Delphi Technique. Open-ended questions are inappropriate when forced-response categories are needed to clarify some point.

Tabulating and quantifying results, and determining meaningful generalizations, tend to be more difficult when using open-ended questions. These questions require a more complex and more subjective coding system than do forced-response questions. Tabulating open-ended results involves examining each respondent's answers on an individual basis. Categories for some characteristic of the responses must also be developed, and each of the open-ended responses is then classified into one of the appropriate categories. In contrast, the categories for classifying forced-response questions are already developed by virtue of the response patterns provided by the respondents. In some cases, the investigator can combine both types of questions.

Open-ended questions can identify topics that a staff-development committee might not have generated. Thus, respondents identify needs, problems, or concerns that can later be translated into forced-response questions. Open-ended questions can be asked in either personal or telephone interviews, or in mailed surveys. Figure 3.1 shows several different examples of open-ended questions that address needs.

Forced-Response Questions. As the term implies, in this question type a respondent can logically select only one category, because the responses are already established and are mutually exclusive. To avoid bias, the question presents an equal number of positive and negative choices. The item should be clearly stated and written as a

---

Figure 3.1

Examples of Open-Ended Questions

When Addressing Teacher Inservice Training

What problems does this school (or district) have in teaching writing?

How do these problems affect you?

What can be done and who can solve the identified problem?

When Addressing Curriculum Needs

What is our most pressing curriculum need in (a) elementary schools, (b) middle schools, (c) high schools?

What do you think contributed to these problems?

What can be done and who can solve the identified problems?

When Addressing Organizational Needs

What policies or procedures are most in need of change to improve the schools?

How do these policies or procedures affect the way in which you do your job?

Who could solve these problems?

---

positive statement. If negative statements are used, respondents quickly become confused.

One of the more commonly used response continuums was developed by Rensis Likert. Note how the following examples use his response patterns; any of these could be used in needs assessments.

More writing experiences are needed in the middle school curriculum.

☐ Strongly Agree   ☐ Disagree
☐ Agree   ☐ Strongly Disagree

I would encourage the school board to promote programs aimed at providing job skills for the physically or mentally disabled.

☐ Encourage Very Much ☐ Discourage
☐ Encourage   ☐ Discourage Very Much
☐ No Opinion

How well do you like attending workshops as compared to other instructional procedures?

- ☐ I like workshops much better.
- ☐ I like workshops a little better.
- ☐ I like all instructional procedures about equally well.
- ☐ I like other instructional procedures a little better than workshops.
- ☐ I like other instructional procedures much better than workshops.

The respondent is requested to select only one category in a Likert-scale item. The categories must be exhaustive and mutually exclusive. These models, as well as other models used here, are provided for your use; feel free to adapt them as you prepare items for needs assessments you conduct.

Figure 3.2 shows a needs survey originally developed by David R. Stronck, which I later adapted. To demonstrate a need for a revised elementary science program in a large school district, the instrument shown here was administered to more than 400 elementary school teachers. Data were tabulated and graphic illustrations were prepared for each item. The results were then appended to a grant application to the National Science Foundation and subsequently the project was awarded $50,000. The needs for that grant were so well documented that the proposal reviewers rated the project higher than one might have expected.

Observe that Figure 3.2 requests three types of information: (1) policy statements, (2) factual statements, and (3) personal judgments. These elements are typically used in any needs assessment to justify a grant. While Figure 3.2 was designed for a grant proposal, it has subsequently been used to determine teachers' perceptions of teaching science as well as other specific subjects. It can easily be adapted to other subjects by dropping the word *science* and substituting some other subject; note how the model questions can easily be generalized.

Rank-Ordered Items. To establish some priority, a rank-ordered set of items helps focus a need. For example, some grant proposal competitions have a fixed limit, say $15,000. In this case, you want to identify those priority

Figure 3.2
Elementary Science Needs Survey

Please indicate the grade level(s) in which you teach science classes
_____ . On the scale at the right, please circle the number that best
describes the intensity of your reaction to each of the questions.

	1=Strongly Disagree	6=Strongly Agree

Children in my school enjoy science.   1 2 3 4 5 6

My school has excellent materials for scientific
activities.   1 2 3 4 5 6

Children in my school would like more
hands-on activities in science.   1 2 3 4 5 6

Our school district should adopt an
activity-centered science program.   1 2 3 4 5 6

My school has excellent texts for studying science.   1 2 3 4 5 6

Our school district should adopt a textbook-
oriented science program at my grade level.   1 2 3 4 5 6

My preparation in science courses is strong.   1 2 3 4 5 6

My preparation in science methods courses
is strong.   1 2 3 4 5 6

An inservice training program for teachers should
be provided when the district is adopting a
new science program.   1 2 3 4 5 6

If an intensive inservice program could be
provided during the summer,
I would be interested in attending.   1 2 3 4 5 6

Our school district should establish a system
for maintaining and distributing living and
consumable materials, which are used in
elementary-science instruction.   1 2 3 4 5 6

Please place any other comments on the reverse side.

N.B. As shown, the items are only end-anchored. That means that only
numbers six and one are explicitly described. To anchor all items, a
descriptor should be included, for example, Disagree=2; Moderately
Disagree=3; Moderately Agree=4; Agree=5.

areas that have a well-designed, quality program or inservice offering for that amount. By comparing the various subgroups of participants, you could quickly evaluate the top priority where funds would be most prudently invested. See Figure 3.3 for an example of the rank-ordering technique. Recognize that the items being ranked are selected by some committee, or perhaps a focus group.

A Discrepancy Model

Needs-assessment designers often use a discrepancy analysis as an alternative technique. A discrepancy exists when respondents perceive that "what ought to take place"

Figure 3.3
Rank-Ordered Items Technique

Below is a list of inservice items. Please rank them from 1 to 9. The highest priority should be ranked 1, the second highest 2, and so on, with 9 being the lowest priority. These items are submitted to you so that the school district staff-development task force can plan for the next year.

Rank

_____ A. Districtwide workshops conducted to give awareness about the NCTM Standards.

_____ B. Inservice programs organized for selected teachers on teaching mathematics problem solving.

_____ C. Inservice programs to implement the district's new mathematics manipulatives program.

_____ D. Released time allowed for work on mathematics curriculum development.

_____ E. Gifted student program mathematics models for the middle school.

_____ F. Pilot test graphing calculators to be introduced in mathematics classes.

_____ G. Questioning strategies workshop for math teachers at all levels.

_____ H. Small-group tutorial techniques emphasizing mathematics.

_____ I. Cooperative learning techniques for math classes.

---

is different from "what seems to take place" or "what is." For example, in Figure 3.3, the issue being addressed concerns a mathematics program. We can convert the items into a discrepancy model by requesting two distinct sets of responses. The first concerns present practices; the second reflects the desired or ideal conditions. Where discrepancies are observed between these conditions, a need exists.

Examine Figure 3.4. In that example, try to determine the most pressing needs relating to mathematics. Obviously, you present rather specific items to be judged. Scoring items is done by averaging each response alone. If item one, "what is" has an average of 3.0, and "what ought to be" is also 3.0, the difference is zero; no discrepancy for that item, the need is being met. If "what is" were 1.0 and "what ought to be" were 4.0, the discrepancy is negative 3.0. This is clearly a pressing need. On the other hand, if "what is" were 4.0 and "ought" were 1.0, there would be a positive value of 3.0. This condition is being overmet. You could even conclude that too much emphasis is being placed on that specific item.

The New York State Education Department (NYSED) has been involved in Comprehensive School Improvement Planning (CSIP) since 1979. Subsequently, the state formulated the Effective Schools Consortia to facilitate change in New York schools based on effective schools research. This is a site-based management, school improvement program that has as one of its major goals the foresight to provide planning teams with proper tools to assess and prioritize needs in areas that have been identified by effective schools research. One of the primary tenets of effective schools research is that clear data drive the entire process. As an example, in 1988, a "Survey of Professional Staff Perceptions of School Programs" was developed to allow building planning teams to gather systematic data for curriculum or program improvement. Data from the survey allowed staff to directly assess the program or process. The set of needs that were identified and prioritized as a result of the survey, as well as the improvement strategies deemed necessary for successful change, were all unique to that school. The individual school is the unit for change.

According to Thomas F. Kelly (1991), one of the architects of the Effective Schools Consortia, organizational

---

Figure 3.4
Discrepancy Model Needs Assessment:
Inservice Questionnaire

Please respond twice for each statement listed in the center. In the left column, labeled "What Is," circle the number that indicates your perception of the current circumstances in your school or district. Then circle one number in the right column, "What Ought To Be."

1 = I strongly disagree
2 = I disagree
3 = I agree
4 = I strongly agree

What Is	Statement	What Ought To Be
1 2 3 4	1. Teachers are offered districtwide awareness workshops about NCTM Standards.	1 2 3 4
1 2 3 4	2. Inservice programs are set up for selected teachers on the teaching of mathematics problem solving.	1 2 3 4
1 2 3 4	3. Staff programs are offered to implement the district's new mathematics manipulatives program.	1 2 3 4
1 2 3 4	4. Teachers need a pilot project to introduce graphing calculators in mathematics classes.	1 2 3 4
1 2 3 4	5. Small-group tutorial techniques are used emphasizing mathematics.	1 2 3 4
1 2 3 4	6. Cooperative learning techniques are used in math classes.	1 2 3 4

improvement cannot happen on a systematic basis without good measurement or assessment. Kelly asserts that the most effective form of assessment is self-assessment. That is why site-based management is built into the New York program.

Kelly notes that most needs assessment instruments are not needs assessment instruments at all. A need is defined as the difference between "what is" and "what should be" (noting a discrepancy). Kelly found that most needs assessment instruments have only one response scale for scoring. If a questionnaire were to ask one to agree or disagree if "teachers should use graphing calculators," does this establish need? Or, is it just an opinion or perception of the stated question? The improper use of assessment instruments makes it nearly impossible to focus on what is truly needed and to prioritize those needs. If a change in the system has been deemed necessary, it should be justified by clear data. This rids the system of personal opinions and emphasizes the data being collected and interpreted. An example of Kelly's basic discrepancy model is shown in Figure 3.5.

Each of the questions in Figure 3.5 is rated for importance and existence. All data are tabulated and mean values for importance and existence are calculated for each question and for each category. If the mean value resulting from the subtraction of importance from existence is negative, then a discrepancy exists at that point. If the value is positive, then there is no discrepancy. Discrepancy values are ordered from most discrepant to least discrepant. This makes it visually easy to identify which category or criterion has a greater need than another.

The Delphi Technique

The preceding sections emphasized the basics of needs-assessment construction: communication, precision, objectivity, simplicity, clarity. The designs of the instruments just discussed are rather traditional. Other information-gathering techniques exist that may be of value as alternative models for, or as components of, a needs assessment. The Delphi Technique is one of them. It has emerged as an excellent method for determining valued or desirable requirements lacking in the schools.

The Delphi Technique was developed and popularized by the RAND Corporation (Helmer 1967). RAND originated the system as a method of identifying group opinions, initially about defense needs, and named it Delphi after the great oracle of Apollo. Basically, the respondents participate in three or more rounds of needs surveying in which they receive their own data, and the data for the entire group, prior to each round. Delphi provides a continuous feedback system to all participants through a privileged design. Each respondent knows how he or she

Figure 3.5
Kelly's Discrepancy Model

Please answer the two questions relating to "importance" and "existence" about each statement. Responses should be based on perceptions that come from personal experiences.

Importance. From your professional viewpoint, how important is this statement in the education of students in your school? In Column A, indicate the *degree of importance* by circling one response in the 5-point scale as follows:

1   Not Important

2   Somewhat Important

3   Important

4   Very Important

5   Priority

Existence. At what level of frequency does the condition as stated exist in your school? In Column B, indicate the existence by circling one response in the 5-point scale as follows:

1   Never

2   Rare

3   Sometimes

4   Usually

5   Always

	Questions	A Importance	B Existence
1.	The mathematics curriculum is defined in terms of outcomes.	1 2 3 4 5	1 2 3 4 5
2.	The mathematics outcomes, curriculum, and materials are congruent.	1 2 3 4 5	1 2 3 4 5
3.	The mathematics curriculum is sequential.	1 2 3 4 5	1 2 3 4 5
4.	The mathematics curriculum provides repetition for learning not demonstrated.	1 2 3 4 5	1 2 3 4 5

Source: Kelly, T.F. (1991). *Practical Strategies for School Improvement.* Wheeling, Ill.: National School Services.

responded, but does not know how any other individual responded. As such, the Delphi Technique allows professional judgments to be made, avoids personality conflicts and interpersonal politics, and reduces the possibility of high-position people from forcing judgments in group discussions in the direction they deem desirable. The Delphi Technique is one means of identifying organizational consensus, determining problem areas, and establishing priorities by providing detailed feedback and systematic follow-up.

One of the problems in making decisions is predicting what the future will hold. It may, therefore, be prudent to establish priorities for goals that have already been identified through other needs assessments, opinionnaires, or small-group task techniques. To this end, the Delphi Technique provides a methodology for organizing and prioritizing the collective judgments of the polled group, or of those who are concerned with planning and crafting a grant proposal.

In the Delphi Technique, the initial procedure is to prepare and distribute a series of questions or problem statements for evaluation. For example, a grant proposal planner might distribute a questionnaire that contains a series of problems, statements, opinions, activities, or predictions of future probabilities. In the first round, respondents provide a rank ordering, a priority, or an evaluation of each item. One modification of this first step is to prepare a general statement eliciting specific responses that can ultimately be converted to items for judging.

All selected participants then receive a second list of items and are asked to either rate the list by selected criteria or reevaluate their original list in reaction to the responses of others provided in the initial ranking. Depending on the method used in the initial round, the lists are returned to each respondent with detailed group rankings plus adverse comments, new ideas for consideration, and minority reports. Typically, the group mean or mode per item is computed and fed back to all participants.

The tabulator of the instruments (a list of rankings in this case) reanalyzes the data and prepares yet a third instrument for distribution to the selected sample. This procedure continues through at least four rankings. By working with multiple submissions of the same set of data, each respondent reaffirms original opinions, modifies some, or adds additional needs to the list. The technique aids in forming a clearly defined convergence pattern of major needs, plus a well-outlined minority opinion.

The Delphi Technique is easily adaptable to needs-assessment surveys designed to analyze the desirability of innovative programs or projects and to justify the need for a grant proposal. A series of needs, for example, might be rated as to their significance. In addition, all respondents are encouraged to provide statements about the impact that the programs might have if instituted. For example, the Delphi Technique is most effective when initially determining whether a group can identify issues, concerns, problems, or suggested courses of action.

Another organizational problem—the formulation of educational policies and plans that allow for alternative future options—can be solved by Delphi analyses. In such cases, preference statements can be written by a task force. The list can then be distributed to the selected subgroup for their initial responses. The complete Delphi Technique then follows. Consensus can easily be identified for those items that have higher or lower means, or modes.

The Delphi Technique is a feedback mechanism allowing selected members of an organization to have an effect in shaping organizational goals and policies. It is very systematic and provides yet another technique for obtaining data for the needs section of a grant proposal.

Focus Groups

The final needs assessment technique that we'll examine is one adapted from market research, the old tool of business entrepreneurs. In reality, focus groups are essentially group interviews where the dynamics of group interaction help stimulate creative responses to problems or issues being resolved. Focus groups are neither formed to solve a problem nor to arrive at a consensus on some topic. The goal is to stimulate discussion and generate a wide spectrum of needs. Typically, individuals are selected who have some characteristic in common for the topic being presented. To continue using the mathematics needs example, such a group would have a range of math teachers, other teachers, persons who apply math, and perhaps a math professor. The focus group leaders should have experience working with groups of six to eight. Only a few open-ended questions are presented to create the stimulus for the group discussion. The technique has proven to be excellent in clarifying issues; providing ideas, perceptions, and assessments; identifying specific problems or needs; and providing feedback quickly. The group leader may tape the discussions or use a recorder who lists key points made by participants to the specific questions. The entire process takes from one to three hours. Then the work begins for the leader and recorder. They must analyze the results along at least four lines: (1) findings, (2) interpretations, (3) value of findings, and (4) recommenda-tions. The needs assessment is summarized and presented to the proposal writing team. Focus groups can also be used to initiate other forms of needs assessment or to corroborate other data.

You might be thinking to yourself, "All I wanted was a few pointers on how to construct the needs section of a grant proposal and I got the whole course on the topic." Well, not really, but the needs assessment and needs section set the stage for your proposal. A strong data-driven needs statement will hold the reviewers' attention, and when you show the significance of the project to some targeted group, you may just have the reviewers leaning toward your corner.

Checklist for Needs Assessment

1. Information on needs is collected systematically.

2. Needs assessments are keyed to specific groups within the organization.

3. Local resources are assessed.

4. Student outcomes are examined critically to determine specific priorities for inservice projects.

5. Delphi or similar techniques are used to arrive at a consensus when prioritizing projects.

6. Discrepancy analyses are used to judge needs.

7. Appropriate literature, which relates to anticipated projects, is reviewed.

8. Needs assessments lead to programs for targeted groups.

9. The significance of the project is explicitly stated.

4
Beginning Elements of the Proposal

YOU NOW HAVE A FIRM GRASP OF WHAT YOU WANT FUNDED. AMONG your stored documents are the needs statements, basic problem, one or two highly probable funders, and support from your team members and significant administrator. (You might even be the significant administrator.) It is now time to begin crafting and constructing the proposal. The first thing I do at this point is bring out the guidelines and examine them in detail.

Guidelines

Smaller foundations may not have guidelines, while large organizations such as the National Institutes of Health may distribute a massive packet of guidelines. Agencies and foundations issue guidelines to bring organizational uniformity to all applications. You should be thoroughly familiar with them. I take a highlighter pen and highlight every important element in the guidelines I'm given.

General Elements: The Feds

For the most part, guidelines are the blueprints you must follow in preparing the full proposal or preproposal. Figure 4.1 is an actual reproduction of the guidelines section issued April 1995 in the U.S. Department of Education Request for Applications (RFA) under the Dwight D. Eisenhower Federal Activities Program, Professional Development, CFDA No. 84.168E. (Remember the CFDA? Yes, it is identified in the RFA.)

Figure 4.1
Dwight D. Eisenhower Guidelines

PART III: APPLICATION PROGRAM NARRATIVE
Before preparing the Application Program Narrative, an applicant should read carefully the notice of final priority, the program description, and the selection criteria used to evaluate applications (see pages C and E1-E3). Listed below are the requested components.

ABSTRACT: Attach a one-page abstract following the Federal Assistance Face Sheet, Form 424. This is a key element in all proposed narratives and should include statements about (1) the need for the project; (2) the proposed plan of operation; and (3) the project's intended outcomes.

PROGRAM NARRATIVE: While there is no required format, applicants are encouraged to prepare the program narrative by addressing the selection criteria in the order listed.

    Meeting purposes of authorizing statute

    Extent of need for project

    Plan of operation

    Quality of key personnel

    Budget and cost-effectiveness

    Evaluation plan

    Adequacy of resources.

LIMITATION ON LENGTH OF APPLICATION PROGRAM NARRATIVE: The applicant must limit the application program narrative to no more than 25 double-spaced, standard typed pages (on one side only), excluding appendices, with one-inch margins. If using a proportional computer font, use no smaller than a 12-point font. If using a non-proportional computer font or a typewriter, do not use more than 10 characters to the inch. **Proposal narratives that exceed this page limit, or narratives using a smaller print size or spacing that makes the narrative exceed the equivalent of this limit, *will not be considered for funding.***

In addition to the information requested in Figure 4.1, there were also pages of forms, legal descriptions, and assurances totaling a stack of paper 4 milimeters thick. As you review the guidelines note the order of items requested and the explicit directions about the proposal document.

The National Science Foundation provides a general set of guidelines requesting the following elements in sequential order:

Cover Sheet
Project Summary
Table of Contents
Project Description—Objectives, Work Goals, Methods
Results from Prior NSF Support
Bibliography
Biographical Sketches
Budget
Current and Pending Support
Facilities, Equipment
Special Information
Appendices

Of course, all of the above are detailed with copious forms in a 68-page booklet. You absolutely must have the guidelines from any federal agency if you want to be successful. And what of the private sector?

Foundation Guidelines

In Chapter 2, I discussed some of the elements needed to contact foundations. To elaborate on that information, I have carefully selected the basic guidelines of four U.S. foundations. This is a fair representation of what the other 37,000 require in the way of an application.

The Bullitt Foundation was founded by a family very concerned with the environment. The family fortune came initially from the forest industry, and later, telecommunications. The Foundation report lists seven program priorities for which they will fund projects: The Puget Sound Area, Columbia River Basin, Open Space, Northwest Forests, Energy and Transportation, Environmental Justice, and Other Environmental Concerns. Applicants must first complete a cover sheet that "includes measurable goals" relating to the funding priorities, and then provide a five-page maximum project description that defends "The significance of the initiative and prospects for success." (Recall my comments that philanthropists have been successful businesspeople and look for winners. The above certainly validates that comment.) Next, a work plan and timetable must be submitted along with a brief history of the applicant's organizational accomplishments and why it can meet the stated need. Finally, a list of personnel, officials of the organization, and the IRS 501(c)(3) verification and IRS 990-PF report are required. There are no surprises here.

The W.K. Kellogg Foundation (made famous by corn flakes) lists six priority areas for funding: health, agriculture, education, philanthropy and volunteerism, leadership, and emergent programming opportunities. The foundation has current assets of $929,736,810. How do you get your share? Figure 4.2 is a direct quote from their annual report.

In Chapter 2, I mentioned the John D. and Catherine T. MacArthur Foundation with assets in excess of $2.95 billion (not bad for a kid selling insurance). According to its guidelines, awards are made in eight areas. The literature also states they do not accept applications for selected areas—they seek them. Brochures with applications are also available for 10 different programs. This foundation

---

Figure 4.2
W.K. Kellogg Application Procedure

The Foundation does not have grant application forms. To be considered for Foundation aid, an institution or organization should write a **one or two-page pre-proposal letter that describes the basic problem and the plan for its solution**. The letter should briefly explain project objectives, operational procedures, time schedules, and personnel and financial resources available and needed. At this preliminary stage personal visits to the Foundation are discouraged.

Pre-proposal letters are carefully evaluated by the Foundation. If the idea is within the Foundation's guidelines and interests, and if Foundation priorities and resources permit consideration of the requested aid, conferences and staff investigation may follow. The organization may be asked to develop a more detailed proposal, which includes a plan for evaluation of the project's effect. In addition to the expertise of its own professional program staff, the Foundation may seek counsel from advisory committees and individual consultants.

Pre-proposal letters are given prompt consideration and should be addressed to:

> Manager of Grant Proposals
> W.K. Kellogg Foundation
> One Michigan Avenue East
> Battle Creek, Michigan 49017-4058
> USA

simply wants an initial letter that does not exceed two or three pages. You should include the following:

Purpose
Problem or issue and its significance
How the project addresses the issue
Qualification to do the work
Relevance to MacArthur's initiatives
Dissemination plan
Budget and total request

Information may be obtained from: The John D. and Catherine T. MacArthur Foundation, 140 South Dearborn Street, Chicago, Illinois 60634.

Carnegie Corporation of New York uses an almost identical format. In 1900, when Andrew Carnegie sold his steel empire to J.P. Morgan, he had a $400 million bank balance. Carnegie's *The Gospel of Wealth* (1889) admonishes the wealthy that they have a "moral obligation" to share their fortunes after they care for all their basic needs. The Foundation now has total assets of $1.11 billion. The Carnegie Guidelines caution that approximately 75 percent of their awards are for renewals. This leaves about 25 percent for new projects. (Recall my note about asking program officers this question.) Carnegie has no deadlines and typically responds in four months. No need to belabor the point; if there are guidelines, get them, follow them carefully, and most will follow the generic model illustrated in this book.

Objectives_____

Depending on the guidelines, you will need a vision statement or a statement of goals. A goal is not a specific action or objective; it is a broad framework. Goals are abstractions that inspire and guide actions. They are seldom attained; objectives often are. One broad goal for schools is "to foster critical thinking." This goal requires that issues be studied and values discussed openly. There is no guarantee it will be achieved. "Goal" is usually used interchangeably with "aims," "purpose," and "long-range outlook."

An objective, on the other hand, describes exactly what will happen, be accomplished, or take place. Every grant proposal requires a set of objectives. Further, objectives must be perfectly aligned with the problem or need that is established. I suggest the following lead: *The objectives of this proposal are to. . . .* This forces you to provide a complete thought. Personally, I do not like a series of incomplete sentences introduced with bullets. A set of objectives from a small grant addressing the need to educate teachers on the use of portfolio assessment follows.

The objectives of the proposal are to:
Implement an across-the-curriculum portfolio model in grades K-5.

Provide working knowledge to the staff about portfolio assessment models so they may select appropriate ones to meet our specific needs.

Focus the staff on student strengths and growth through portfolio assessments.

Provide a model for long-term assessment of student learning.

Another example comes from a study of the occupational aspirations of women. It had two objectives:

This study will compare the differential effects of attending college upon the educational and occupational aspirations of men and women.

The second objective is to test levels of aspiration via two theoretical structures: "relative deprivation" and "environmental press."

The next model has a goal statement followed by four specific objectives.

Goal: The proposal has two goals. The first is to provide a preservice model that can be easily disseminated, adapted, and implemented in not only land-grant universities, but in all universities having a similar administrative organization. The second is to redress the collectively identified science deficiencies in teacher preparation existing nationally as well as on our own campus.

Objectives: The objectives of this proposal are to

1. Design a physical science course for elementary majors with the intent of constructing a national model.

2. Integrate scientific epistemology and relevant science history within the science context.

3. Design appropriate laboratory activities.

4. Integrate modern media, (e.g., video disk and microcomputers) into the program.

The next two examples show that you need not follow one formula or lead-in to specify proposal objectives.

Objectives of the Clinical Trial: It is hypothesized that estrogen replacement therapy (ERT) will reduce the risk of coronary disease and of osteoporosis-related fractures. Because progestin and estrogen replacement therapies (PERT) are commonly used together in order to diminish the risk of endometrial cancer, a PERT arm will be included to assess whether the hypothesized beneficial effects on preventing coronary disease and fractures will be retained. The incidence of endometrial cancer and breast cancer will be monitored during and after the trial. The estimated sample size requirement for the outcome of this coronary heart disease is 25,000. This sample size would give a power of 94 percent for detecting a 30 percent reduction in CHD incidence over nine (9) years.

Dietary modification in the form of a low-fat eating pattern is hypothesized to reduce the risk of breast cancer, colorectal cancer, and coronary heart disease. The estimated sample size requirement for each of the outcomes of breast cancer and colorectal cancer is 48,000. The sample size gives a power of 81 percent for detecting a 15 percent reduction in breast cancer, and 94 percent power for detecting a 21 percent reduction in colorectal cancer incidence over nine (9) years.

Another model shows an even more diverse way of incorporating the aim, rationale, and objectives. Notice that each statement begins with an action verb.

The primary aim of this research is to interface engineering technology with the field of cytapheresis research by investigating and developing an online approach to blood separator optimization. The method will take advantage of fundamental settling characteristics of cellular particles by adjusting cell concentrations with separated fraction recycle. Additional benefits of this effort will be that the optimizations will be accomplished without cell sedimenting agents and that cellular species in separated fractions will be determined online. To accomplish these tasks, the following specific objectives will be pursued:

Interface an online computer system to a cell counting system, an automated sampling system, and an existing cell centrifuge. This will allow current information about the centrifuge to be collected and analyzed with the computer, as well as allowing the computer to control and optimize the operation of the centrifuge.

Combine the separation of blood at reduced HCT with recycle techniques to extend initial examinations of the basic sedimentation character of cellular species and clarify optimum operating modes of the centrifuge.

Investigate and develop an online optimization technique for the cell centrifuge which will predict the degree of separation as a function of operating parameters and change the operating parameters so that the maximum separation efficiency is obtained at all times.

Develop a method, using a Coulter counter interfaced with the laboratory computer, to estimate the total number of cells collected during a procedure.

Perform experiments to implement, test, and verify the proposed online optimization technique.

Some guidelines will request a measurable objective or outcome. Assume that the goal of the project is to prepare bilingual tutors. You must write a measurable objective. It might read as:

After completion of the four-week ESL training program, 90 percent of the 20 trainees will be employed in the area's public schools as teacher aides or student tutors.

This type of objective is extremely specific. Use it only if requested, because you cannot control the conditions necessary for success.

Conditions About Objectives

A common error in stating objectives is to list too many. Keep the number of objectives to a manageable size. I was on a panel where one proposal listed 10 needs, 9 outcomes, and 16 objectives. Another had three broad goals and four value assumptions. These were not funded. In the former, the World Bank could not have funded it, and in the latter, the seven statements detracted from the needs.

Five is an optimum number of objectives to include in a proposal, yet it is not uncommon in large proposals or those that are multiyear to have several objectives. How do you reconcile this situation? You divide the objectives into subgroups and for each subgroup you state an overarching goal. In this manner, you not only show good organization, you illustrate that complex projects can be made more manageable.

Another common error in stating objectives is to combine the objective with the means by which you will attain it. These complex statements are usually very lengthy and only confuse panel members as they read them. Restating the need or problem as an objective is another common mistake. Remember, the need is a condition; the problem is a statement being proposed for solution. Some proposal writers begin discussing a unique feature of the project and never write an objective at all.

Once you write the objectives, you have the vital elements of your blueprint and can begin to add the details on how you will complete each one.

Conducting a Literature Search for Grant Proposals_____

A literature search examines sources of information on a given subject that exist in several places and in various forms to obtain background information in providing the rationale for a proposal or research design. Such information may be obtained from published articles, funded proposals, and equipment catalogs, or through personal communications. As implied, all references need not be of a printed nature (e.g., telephone conversations or interviews). They need to be verifiable, however, and careful notes should be made of nonprint sources. The literature search is usually done after the need for a proposed action is explored. Seek advice from colleagues or others engaged in related activities to determine feasibility and interest.

Purposes of a Literature Search

There are three main purposes of a literature search. The first is to acquaint the reader with (a) existing studies relative to what is being proposed, (b) those who have done similar work, (c) dates and locations of the latest studies, and (d) approaches involving methodology, instrumentation, and statistical analyses that were followed. The second is to establish a possible need for the proposed project and the likelihood for obtaining meaningful, relevant, and significant results. You show that your idea works, is sound, and is also different. The third purpose is to provide a conceptual framework for developing a rationale for the proposed project.

Important Sources

General references such as the *Review of Educational Research* or *Psychological Bulletin* contain summaries of previous work related to a given situation or research problem. Seek the most prestigious journals in your area. Look for research, not opinions. Specific books, monographs, bulletins, reports, and research articles— preferably those written very recently—are all useful.

Unpublished materials (e.g., dissertations, theses, and papers presented at recent professional meetings), possibly available through sources such as ERIC, are excellent. Often, the most recent studies will be refereed papers given at professional meetings. Government publications, previously funded proposals, and reports from funding agencies about similar projects are great sources. Using published studies from a funding agency will impress the program officer that you know their material.

Make a preliminary review of the subject so you understand terminology, background, and limitations of published studies. To find more sources, refer to the citations in the most important studies and check them for further leads. Continue the process until there is an overlap among cited articles. This technique is called a "fan search," since each paper contains a bibliography that spreads out like a fan. As you conduct the literature search, stay focused. Tempting as it may be, do not go off on tangents. Your review has to have a tight focus that supports your objectives and plan of operation.

Use primary sources for your key references. Keep in mind, the length of your proposal will be limited. Currently, the average is about 15 pages single spaced. A review of literature should be about 1 page, or at maximum, 2 pages of the total 15.

Presenting the Findings

Once you organize the literature, summarize key points; select and arrange it in a manner that is parallel with your own format. For example, if you state questions, hypotheses, or specific aims, structure the literature in the same order. An organized structure will help reviewers, and you'll receive winning points if they do not have to reread previous sections. Highlight critical information, but do not list an entire line with citations for some self-evident point. Laundry lists of citations detract from points being made. Don't cite extensive passages unless the original writer stated it so profoundly that the key will be missed if you paraphrase.

The nature of a proposal will determine whether or not a literature search is needed and how extensive it should be. For a basic research proposal, for example, a rigorous and exhaustive literature search may be required. When preparing a proposal for the purchase of a single piece of instructional scientific equipment, it may be sufficient to indicate that the most recent equipment catalog was used to obtain the cost and description of the equipment requested.

The need to contain evidence of a literature search varies with each proposal. When proposing the purchase and use of computer equipment for instructional purposes, give a clear rationale for how you decided to purchase the particular piece of equipment. Such a decision should be based on the successful use of such equipment under similar circumstances at other institutions. Similarly, the use of new educational techniques and technologies, such as Computer-Assisted Instruction (CAI), or Personalized System of Instruction (PSI), should be well documented with evidence that they are appropriate for the local setting. See Appendix B for one model of a literature review focused on the project's aim.

A Summary as a Working Blueprint

One helpful device that we use in nearly all episodes of preparing grant proposals is the project summary or abstract. This short document briefly lists the need, objectives, general statement of procedures, and evaluation. We craft this piece to help the writing team members. Everyone knows what is being planned. Of course, this statement will be rewritten two, three, or four times to accurately reflect the whole project.

Keep in mind that the summary often will be the very first page read by the reviewers. You want it to read perfectly. Refine it. Rewrite it. Edit it. Make certain it says what you want to say in precisely the right words. Word selection is critical. A proposal faces its most important evaluation when the reviewer reads that statement.

In keeping with the idea that you should be exposed to several different forms, I illustrate three in the following figures and close with two more checklists for your use.

**Figure 4.3
Plant Research**

The overall objectives of this research are to fully understand the chemical nature of the systemic response of plants to pest attacks or wounding that results in the regulation of expression of proteinase inhibitor genes. More specifically, research is planned to (1) identify, isolate, and characterize the chemical signal(s) that is (are) released and transported throughout tomato plants in response to wounding; (2) determine the mechanism(s) by which the systemic wound signals are released; (3) determine the mechanism(s) of signal reception in target cells and determine the nature of the intracellular mechanism that results in the regulation of expression of proteinase inhibitor genes.

Figure 4.4

**State Budgeting for Higher Education
Practice and Theory**

Objectives: State budget formulation is an important process that is seriously lacking documentation. State budgeting agencies are under heavy pressure to improve budget practice in relation to higher education, despite uncertainties surrounding the effectiveness of existing budgeting techniques and policy formulation. The increasing competition for state revenue, the lack of increases in productivity, the redistribution of enrollments among institutions, the demands for cost and productivity information, and the incongruity between educational expectations and available resources—all place strains on the budgeting process.
Information regarding this process is scattered and not readily available. Therefore, the major objective of this study is to provide information and guidelines to improve state budget formulations for post-secondary educations. A second objective is to test certain theoretical concepts in interorganizational cooperation, Program Planning and Budgeting Systems, Management by Objectives, and others in order to develop a theory about resource allocation processes.

Methods and Procedures: The study will conduct a field investigation in 18 states supplemented by a questionnaire survey of all 50 states. Selected propositions of organizational theory will be tested with data collected in the field investigation. The study is a three-year effort that will provide state level policymakers with a broad perspective of budget formulation across all of its elements. The project will provide the context for later, more informed assessments of the separate elements of budget formulation.

Significance: The information and guidelines developed from this study will play an important role in building a state system for the delivery of career education. This system is to be one of the priorities for career education during the next few years. It will include post-secondary education as one of its elements, and a thorough knowledge of state budgeting policies and practices for higher education is a necessary component of the total system. The estimated cost is $341,620.

Figure 4.5
A Statewide System to Promote the Implementation of New Programs in Science, Mathematics, and Social Studies

Project Director: Donald C. Orlich
Estimated Cost: $25,000 each year

The Problem: There is a need to provide a prototype system for a statewide mechanism to diffuse curricular innovations in elementary and middle school science, mathematics, and social sciences. This need would be reduced by coordinating the plans, activities, and structures of four already existing agencies: The National Science Foundation, Washington State University, The Washington Office of the State Superintendent of Public Instruction, and the Washington Educational Service Districts (ESD's), which encompass the state's 296 operating school districts.

Objectives: The specific objectives of this project are to:

1. Provide intensive preparation during the summer to curriculum specialists selected by the Washington Educational Service Districts to create resource personnel for "Science—A Process Approach" (SAPA), "Science Curriculum Improvement Study" (SCIS), and "Elementary School Science" (ESS). Six other programs will be selected for the subsequent summers.

2. Provide each resource person with sets of diffusion strategies and paradigms for presenting inservice orientation programs on the selected curricula in the respective educational service districts.

3. Establish and evaluate a model for a statewide dissemination and diffusion network.

Procedures: A series of three intensive summer workshops will be conducted on campus at WSU. Participants in these resource personnel workshops will be curriculum specialists designated by the ESD's. The resource persons will be prepared to understand the rationale, structure, and materials of each program and will return to the respective ESD's to conduct a series of awareness-information workshops on the programs. An evaluation of the system will be concurrently conducted through use of data collecting instruments to determine the number of awareness workshops conducted and the number of adoptions of "new" programs.

Significance of Project: This system could be a prototype model for other states. The plan is conceptually similar to the change-agent model which has been so effective in the nation's agricultural sector.

Introduction/Problem/Objectives Checklist

Circle the letter to the left that best describes your evaluation of that element. Anything less than "top" rating should be followed by a written statement to help the writer improve.

Introduction
1. The initial statements provide:
   a. Very smooth transition for the reader
   b. An implied transition
   c. Some disconnectedness
   d. Some confusion
2. The introductory paragraph:
   a. Provides a general idea to the reader
   b. Leads the reader to the problem
   c. Seems choppy
   d. Seems to be abrupt
3. The introduction *as written*:
   a. Is well crafted
   b. Needs some editing
   c. Needs major rewriting
   d. Detracts from the problem

Problem or Need
1. Significance of the problem *as written*:
   a. Rather significant
   b. Moderately significant
   c. Rather insignificant
   d. Very insignificant
2. Clarity of statement of the problem:
   a. Very clear
   b. Rather clear
   c. Somewhat ambiguous
   d. Rather obscure
3. Documentation is provided or cited to substantiate the problem or need:
   a. Citations or data provided
   b. Some data given
   c. Implied, but not cited
   d. No documentation
4. The problem section is stated:
   a. Explicitly
   b. Somewhat explicitly, but needs focus

c. Somewhat inexplicitly
d. Very inexplicitly

Objectives
1. Relationship of the objectives to the stated problem:
   a. Well integrated
   b. Moderately integrated
   c. Incomplete
   d. Reflects lack of precision
2. Extent to which objectives are clearly or succinctly stated:
   a. Very clear
   b. Rather clear, but some revisions needed
   c. Too wordy
   d. Obscure
3. The number of objectives seem to be:
   a. Adequate
   b. In need of some recombining
   c. Somewhat redundant
   e. Excessive
4. My overall rating of the objectives section is:
   a. Excellent
   b. Good
   c. Adequate, but needs polish
   d. Inadequate

Evaluation Checklist for Project Abstracts or Summaries

The numerical rating codes to the right should be interpreted to mean:

NA	Not Applicable to Project
1	Very Inadequately Stated
2	Inadequately Stated
3	Adequately Stated
4	Very Adequately Stated

1. The introduction clearly "sets the stage."		1 2 3 4
2. Problem or need is clearly stated.		1 2 3 4
3. The problem or need is significant within the context of this abstract.		1 2 3 4
4. Objectives are clearly stated.		1 2 3 4
5. Hypotheses are clearly stated.	NA	1 2 3 4
6. Relationship of the problem or needs to previous research is clearly stated.	NA	1 2 3 4
7. Significance of projected results stated.	NA	1 2 3 4
8. Research design is appropriate to problem solution.	NA	1 2 3 4
9. Project procedures are appropriate to problem solution.	NA	1 2 3 4
10. Methods are identified to analyze data.	NA	1 2 3 4
11. Evaluation section focuses on objectives.	NA	1 2 3 4
12. Abstract is clearly written.		1 2 3 4
13. Abstract is logically organized.		1 2 3 4
14. Abstract is written in an unbiased manner.		1 2 3 4
15. Overall ranking of total abstract.		1 2 3 4

5
Procedures, Management, and Evaluation

CRAFTING THE PROPOSAL FOLLOWS A "LOGIC LADDER"—THE NEEDS OR problem statement leads to the objectives, and the objectives lead to the procedures. Each objective is fully amplified in this section of the proposal. This section can be titled "methodology," "work plan," "project activities," or "scope of operation." Label it according to your guidelines. For this discussion, I'll call it procedures.

Procedures

Procedures explain how you will accomplish each objective. To do this, restate each objective and detail the following:

Who will be involved.
What precisely will take place.
When the activities will take place.
Where the activities will take place.
Why this approach is being used.

In some larger proposals, review of literature is interwoven with the specific procedures. For example, if this were an inservice training proposal and you were using the peer-coaching model, you would provide a short review showing the efficacy of that model. In addition, you would address the key functions:

Planning
Organizing human and other resources
Staffing the project
Directing activities
Coordinating project elements
Reporting on various aspects
Budget responsibility

Do you recognize P-O-S-D-CO-R-B, the functional approach to management (Gulick and Urwick 1937)? I always use P-O-S-D-CO-R-B when completing the procedures section because it makes me account for all the functions of successful project management. These details must be addressed in the procedures section. Refer to the model proposal illustrated in Appendix B.

Timelines

In many guidelines, you are asked to prepare a PERT Chart (Program Evaluation Review Technique) or a Gantt chart. These timelines illustrate who is responsible for what and when specific events are scheduled.

To prepare any timeline model, brainstorm with the writing team to identify key tasks. These ideas are sorted and displayed in a logical, chronological order. Figures 5.1, 5.2, and 5.3 contain partially complete timeline formats. I have deliberately not illustrated a PERT chart due to space and art limitations. Desmond L. Cook (1978) has an excellent set of illustrations using PERT charts for a wide variety of projects. His work is an excellent source book.

Staffing

It is imperative that you list all persons who will participate in the project, since in the budget you will be paying for their services. If you do not list staff in the narrative portion of the proposal, you cannot provide a budgeted item for them. I, personally, have all people committed before the proposal is finalized. Some agencies require an actual letter of commitment from personnel listed in the proposal, so plan well in advance.

Observe how personnel are listed in the model proposal in Appendix B. Each person's responsibilities are detailed. Any program officer or review panel member can

---

Figure 5.1
A Partially Completed Activity and Responsibility Chart

Activity	Responsibility	Product
Review Purpose and Goals	Advisory Group	Assignment of Tasks
Literature Search	Project Assistants	Summary of Relevant Articles
Devise Survey Instrument	Project Director and Assts.	Copies for Pretest
Evaluate Instrument	Advisory Group	Suggested Revisions
Distribute Instrument	Project Assistants	Complete Distribution
Process and Analyze Data	Project Director and Assts.	Tallied Results
Write Final Report	Project Director and Assts.	Draft for Review
Seminar on Results	Project Director	Further Dissemination

Figure 5.2

A Partial Timeline for Project Activities

```
    1   3   5   7   9   11  13  15  17  19  21  23  25  27  29  31
Week
      2   4   6   8  10  12  14  16  18  20  22  24  26  28  30  32
TASK #1 ——7————      ——8——    ——9——    ————10Δ
START
  --2--
    ——3——
        ——4——
          ————5————6Δ
```

1. Start-up—September 15
2. Review of Principles
3. Establishment of Formats and Designs
4. Refinement of Steps 2 and 3
5. Selection of Pilot Test Personnel
6. Progress Reported to Agency
7. Preparation of Preliminary Draft for Pilot Testing
8. Administration of Instrument
9. Analysis of Results
10. Preparation and Submission of Final Report

Figure 5.3
Partially Complete GANTT Chart

Descriptors	Year One 2 4 6 8 10 12	Year Two 2 4 6 8 10 12
1. Review of Practices— Project Paper		
Review Literature	___	
Write Paper	_____	
Produce	____	
Distribute	____	
Deliver to NSF	Δ	
2. Teaching Documents Set #1		
Collect Materials	_____	
Review Materials	_____	
Document Exemplary School Practices	_____	
Describe Products (1st Version)	____	
Revise	_____	
Evaluate Document Usefulness	_____	
Produce Documents	_____	
Distribute to Test Sites	____	
Deliver Set to NSF	Δ	

see that much planning has gone into the proposal, and key responsibilities and functions are identified in advance. That is the essence of effective planning.

A vita or resume for key personnel, (i.e., project director, assistant director, and others) should be included. Read your guidelines for the format that should be followed. In general, the vitae should be uniformly organized. In many cases, some project leaders will not have a current vita. If that is so, use Figure 5.4 as a worksheet for standardizing the display of vitae. "Quality of Personnel" is often a major evaluative criterion for judging proposals. Be certain that everyone's strengths, as they apply to the project, are highlighted. Figure 5.4 should be prepared on at least three or four pages, allowing ample space under each main entry for insertions. These

Figure 5.4
Vita Worksheet

PRELIMINARIES
Full Name   Mailing Address
Title   Telephone
Organization   FAX
                                       e-mail

HIGHER EDUCATION
Degree, University, City, Major, Date

NB: Use separate entries for B.A., M.A., Ph.D.

ADDITIONAL EDUCATIONAL EXPERIENCES
Specify post B.A., M.A., or Ph.D. work, special institutes, seminars, and workshops of at least six hours duration. If leaders are known, list them also and be sure to list location. If you attended an invited seminar be certain to note that.

PROFESSIONAL EXPERIENCES
List your occupational records.
Veterans—list service dates.
List date, position, rank or title (most recent to less recent).

PROFESSIONAL AWARDS
List biographies, recognition from professional groups, awards, and prizes. Place modesty aside in this section. All honors that have been received should be listed.

LEADERSHIP POSITIONS AND COMMITTEES
List leadership positions held in all professional organizations. Especially note service on various committees (e.g., curriculum, search, awards, scholarship, and program evaluation committees; and student service clubs advised).

PROFESSIONAL ORGANIZATIONS
Provide a listing of current memberships in all professionally related organizations. If you are a "life member," so note.

PROFESSIONAL ACTIVITIES AND SERVICES
List consultancies, evaluation teams, review panels, addresses delivered, and services you rendered.

PROFESSIONAL PUBLICATIONS
Use a standard bibliographic format and list major or all published works.

GRANTS, PROPOSALS, REPORTS
List only funded grant proposals; give title of grant, funding agency, date, and amount.
Also list proposals pending and reports that you authored or coauthored. The reports need not be published.

worksheets are collected, edited, and prepared in a uniform format for all key players. If you are alone on the project, then you are "chief cook and bottle washer." You need a vita and must describe what you will do.

Evaluation Considerations

All evaluation is subjective. I carefully chose that predicate and did not write *arbitrary, capricious, biased,* or *objective.* Subjective means you determine what should be evaluated, how, and to what magnitude of fidelity. One tip will save you much grief—employ the ladder logic again. The objectives should drive the evaluation; therefore, focus the evaluation on how well you attain the objectives. For example, if your objective is to provide inservice training, then your evaluation model should focus on the participants' opinion of the training and perhaps how much the participants learned as a consequence of the project. If the project is to design and implement some specific materials, then the evaluation should follow that line. Keep the evaluation objective, but also keep it simple. If you have a multiyear, big proposal, then you need a complex evaluation model, but for the most part, you don't.

In addition to evaluating the objectives, I recommend you list a set of questions that will guide the evaluation process. For example, "Do teachers change their instructional methods as a consequence of attending inquiry-oriented workshops?" "How effective are short-term workshops for implementing new programs?" These questions would then be answered by designing appropriate evaluation techniques. Below are a few models and techniques.

Formative and Summative Evaluation

Formative evaluation is most applicable for training or curriculum projects. Michael C. Scriven (1967) initially described the formative evaluation model. It is designed to provide immediate feedback to project directors allowing them to identify and rectify problems during the course of a project. For example, if a particular methodology is being used that causes participants to do poorly, a formative evaluation would check the small steps and identify potentially detrimental learning or instructional problems. Formative strategies are specifically designed to monitor aspects of any group to determine where problems may be emerging. The techniques in this model should be initiated so instructors can observe many different perspectives of a program while it is in operation. This is imperative for carefully sequenced topics or where critical prerequisite skills are being learned. Figure 5.5 illustrates one formative evaluation form I have used in conducting funded workshops since 1972.

Only a few select items need to be checked during any formative evaluation. These are all based on the stated project objectives. You do not need a lengthy list of items. The important point is that the feedback is collected while there is adequate time to make adjustments in the project's operations. The rationale for formative evaluation is to

---

Figure 5.5
Project Feedback

Directions: Place an "X" on each line above the category that best describes your reactions.

1. How has the project progressed to date?

|——|

Moving very slowly   Could move faster   Moving along nicely

2. How is your participation in this project?

|——|

Not with it at all   Could be more involved   Really with it

3. Is the organization and conduct of the project meeting your
   expectations?

|——|

Not at all   Meeting some and   Meeting all and then some
                    not meeting others

4. How adequately will you be able to make an easy adjustment of
   translating the content from this project to your own classes?

|——|

Very inadequately   Inadequately   Adequately   Very adequately

5. Comments or suggestions:

---

provide data for making correctives—immediately, if not sooner. When participants and program staff members realize they are being constantly monitored and helped, they tend to become more responsible and productive. The instructional climate and total environment become positive and supportive. This is precisely the kind of learning climate that one always ought to subscribe when teaching. Conversely, projects have gone on the rocks because the project director was not evaluating project activities over short periods of time and waited until the very end of the project to accomplish a one-shot final evaluation.

Formative evaluation requires the project director to carefully observe a select set of experiences for all participants. For example, with science inservice programs, some form of laboratory activity is used to build a cluster of generic skills for future use. A person using formative evaluation would monitor the skills, and when a participant did poorly, a new set of experiences would be provided. To correct a noted learning deficiency, one does not wait to take the final exam. Correctives are an integral part of the formative evaluation plan.

One simple method for recording formative data is to tabulate the absolute numbers or percentages of both individual and group activities. A project director could compare group data on a graph so that the directions of the groups could be visually displayed for instant analysis. The essential characteristic of a formative evaluation is that "hard data" are being collected to add a more objective evaluation to what is usually considered soft data or the subjective elements of evaluation. More importantly, correctives are built into the scheme so that feedback is used when it is needed most—not stored for the future.

The evaluation conducted as the final or concluding task is called the summative evaluation and might be the final formative evaluation of a project. Summative evaluations may take several forms, just so they are consistent with the prescribed objectives of the program. Summative data could be tabulated into absolute responses and then as a percentage for each item. Comparisons between students could also be made on summative data (but not on the formative measures). Summative test data could then be arranged in a profile to illustrate the sum of evaluation activities. Formative data provide feedback, while the summative scores lead to judgments about the quality of performances.

Most projects fail because evaluation is a one-shot, post-evaluation. Such an evaluation strategy can never aid a project director because the information comes when the project is over. You could argue that formative and summative techniques will cause the direction of the project to change. I agree, and I would submit that if properly used, the objectives of the project might be altered. Success is the underlying tenet of this evaluation technique. If a program, course, or project needs to be modified because of unrealistic expectations (objectives), then why not alter it? If you do alter a stated objective, be sure to contact your funding agency's program officer to receive approval.

Perhaps the most compelling reason in support of the formative and summative model is that there are really no surprises at the end of the project. With early feedback systems built, all elements converge toward success. Figure 5.6 illustrates one successful model.

Achievement Tests

Achievement tests are constructed to assess a participant's terminal behavior or the expected behavior or attainment after completing a project. Achievement tests assess the degree or quality that the desired behavior or performance takes place. Such test scores tend to show a level of current skill development.

Achievement scores provide two types of information: (1) the individual's level of skill or knowledge relative to an established level of quality control, and (2) the relative ordering (rank) of the individual's score in relation to the rest of the class. Robert Glaser (1963) refers to the first type of information as criterion-referenced and states that these measures depend upon an absolute standard of quality. This means that the participant either has or has not acquired the predetermined mastery level of the skill. The degree of skill attainment is usually stated in some descriptive term. The second type of information is usually referred to as norm-referenced, since it compares a student

---

Figure 5.6
Summative Evaluation for Short-Term Workshops

Directions: Please circle the number to the left of each statement that best describes your evaluation of each item.

1 - Totally Inadequate
2 - Poor
3 - Somewhat Positive or
    Somewhat Negative
4 - Good
5 - Excellent

1. The specified goals of the project were: 1 2 3 4 5

2. The climate or atmosphere of the project was: 1 2 3 4 5

3. The overall design of the project was: 1 2 3 4 5

4. The start-up, introductory activities were: 1 2 3 4 5

5. The staff, in terms of concern and awareness
   of the participants, was: 1 2 3 4 5

6. The manner in which the participants could
   influence the direction of the project was: 1 2 3 4 5

7. The use of the staff resources during the
   project was: 1 2 3 4 5

8. The articulation of content to science classes
   during the project was: 1 2 3 4 5

9. The experiential or hands-on activities used
   in the project were: 1 2 3 4 5

10. My overall rating of this project is: 1 2 3 4 5

11. Comments:

---

with other students in a selected group. Glaser says the student's level of achievement occurs somewhere on a hypothetical continuum of knowledge or skill proficiency ranging from zero (e.g., the student cannot balance an oxidation-reduction equation), to mastery (the student can balance all oxidation-reduction equations).

Generally, achievement tests are norm-referenced. For the past few years, however, my colleagues and I have been developing criterion-referenced measures in elementary science. All test items are keyed only to the activities being used. We administer the same pre-test and post-test, compute means and standard deviations, and then compute an effect size to determine the learning gain for participants in the training sessions, as well as students.

The effect size is expressed as a decimal or mixed number. For example, an effect size of 1.0 can be interpreted as a gain of one standard deviation on a normal curve for the treatment group. An effect size of 2.0 is phenomenal. At 0.3, an effect size becomes useful or important. Effect sizes less than 0.2 are usually not important. An effect size of 0.25 begins to show importance.

To calculate the effect size, subtract the mean score of the pre-test from the mean score of the post-test and then divide the difference by the standard deviation of the pre-test. For example, on a post-test assume that the group had a mean of 90, while the mean of the pre-test was 80 with a standard deviation of 8.0 points. The difference of the means, or 10, is divided by 8 for a 1.25 effect size. Stay with that treatment, it's a winner. By the way, many researchers do not report their test scores in such a manner, so one cannot compute an effect size. I wonder why?

For discussions about effect size, see Gene V. Glass (1976 and 1980), Jacob Cohen (1988), Benjamin S. Bloom (1984) and a monumental work that reports dozens of treatments and effect sizes by Herbert J. Walberg (1991).

Other Evaluation Techniques

Depending on the project objectives, there are several other techniques that may be employed to evaluate success. The first is to observe pre- and post-behaviors of the participants. This is a powerful method, especially where new curriculums or teaching methods are being stressed. Observational techniques are, however, labor intensive and thus expensive. The second is to employ participant journals. This strategy approximates a case study or qualitative approach to evaluation. The third technique is judging some product or achievement. Many individuals are funded to produce training tapes, print materials, computer software, or some product. A panel could be used to evaluate these artifacts.

Single subject design (time series) is yet a fourth technique that could be employed as an evaluation model. The initial step is to identify a very specific behavior that is deemed useful or appropriate. Next, you count the times that behavior is displayed by the subject to establish a baseline. An intervention then takes place (e.g., inservice training), a reinforcerer (new materials), followed by more observations. If the data show increases in the desired behavior, then the project is considered to be successful.

I suggest contacting the National Science Foundation to obtain a copy of its recently published monograph on project evaluation, *User-Friendly Handbook for Project Evaluation: Science, Mathematics, Engineering and Technology Education* (Fyechtling 1994). Another handy reference is one compiled by Ernest R. House (1978). House identifies eight major evaluation models and provides a wide array of techniques for evaluating your proposal.

A final evaluation technique is the "third party contract," or placing the evaluation out on bid. The main elements for such a subcontract are as follows:

> Purpose or evaluation questions to be answered.
> Services and products to be provided.
> Qualifications of evaluators.
> Scheduling specifications.
> Evaluation plans.
> Nature of reports.
> Assurances.
> Budget and payment schedule.

A third party subcontract is a good idea when you have a very large grant (in excess of $500,000) and one that is multiyear. The rationale for subcontracting the evaluation is that you have a greater probability of objectivity than if you conduct the evaluation with someone from your organization.

Since procedures are key to any proposal's funding, I've provided a checklist on the next page to judge your procedures section.

Procedures Checklist

Circle the number that describes the component being evaluated.

Key: 1 = Very Inadequate
2 = Inadequate
3 = Adequate
4 = Very Adequate

1. The introduction provides a clear and logical lead to the problem.   1 2 3 4
2. The problem/need is explicitly stated.   1 2 3 4
3. The objectives describe what will take place.   1 2 3 4
4. The procedures relate to the needs or problem.   1 2 3 4
5. The procedures relate to the objectives.   1 2 3 4
6. The procedures explicitly illustrate how each objective will be implemented.   1 2 3 4
7. The procedures show a logical sequencing.   1 2 3 4
8. The procedures, as prepared, show a definite sequence of activities.   1 2 3 4
9. The proposal provides reasons for the selection of the activities.   1 2 3 4
10. My overall rating of the procedures section is: 1 2 3 4

6
Calculating a Budget

Twelve basic principles guide preparation of the proposal budget:

Principle 1. Always follow the guidelines. While this may be redundant, self-evident, or repetitive, it is critical. Carefully examine the costs that are allowed, those that must be matched, and those that are not allowed. A simple examination of the guidelines will alleviate budget renegotiations or just plain rejection.

Principle 2. Never ask for more than you need. We all may have heard how to pad a budget, but quite frankly, padding is an ethically dubious technique. What is your best estimate for each category? Check each with your accounting office and, above all, be absolutely honest about the numbers.

Principle 3. You get what you earn. This means that no matter what you think you are worth, you get exactly the same salary on "soft" money as you do on the "hard" stuff. Salaries cannot be inflated just because somebody else is paying for them.

Principle 4. If it is not in the narrative, it won't get funded. Novice grant proposal writers often assume that simply plugging in a few figures will suffice. No! You must have every activity described in the narrative. You must identify everyone in the proposal who will eventually be paid. Obviously, you won't list every name, but you must identify the job position and what will be done. You can pay for that chartered bus to take the field trip, just be sure the trip is mentioned in the procedures. Program officers will redline any item appearing in the budget that is not documented or identified in the narrative.

Principle 5. Projections are all right. Many fiscal agents use Consumer Price Index figures to predict future salaries. The salary you made this year should be subsequently higher in four years. Establish some projected percentage rates of increase and keep them constant throughout the budget. The budget actually consists of two sections: a tally of figures and the budget justification. The latter requires a rationale for each figure shown on the budget summary sheet.

Principle 6. Don't forget the fringe benefits. If part or all of a salary is being paid by the grant, then so is that proportion of the fringe benefits. For state or private institutions, these are all carefully specified in a master agreement. Some nonprofit organizations, however, need to have an adopted list of fringe benefits so they don't lose money when a grant is awarded, or worse yet, require that you pay out of pocket for them. It is all legitimate. Consider that for many employees the total fringe benefit package exceeds 35 percent of a person's salary.

Principle 7. You get paid in proportion to the work scheduled. If you work on project activities for 25 percent of the academic year, then all you can make from the grant is 25 percent of your salary and fringe benefits.

Principle 8. You only get 100 percent. No matter how you complain or show that you are working 60 hours per week, you only get paid for a 40-hour work week and your grant-paid salary cannot exceed 100 percent of your actual "hard money" salary. In most cases, you may not get paid overtime. There is one exception. If the work being done is above or beyond your regular work assignments, then you may be paid "extra compensation." Those two magic words must be noted in the budget justification in advance. You cannot be paid overtime retroactively.

Principle 9. Designated services are reimbursed. Travel, supplies, materials, per diem, hotels, taxis, long distance costs, services, and rentals are all legitimate budget items. Again, you must list or write these into the narrative. Yes, you can have your grant pay for you to attend the next ASCD convention. You simply add that point in your dissemination section.

Principle 10. Equipment is tough to come by. Sorry, unless that lap-top computer is being used for training, or is thoroughly justified in the narrative, you won't be allowed the purchase from most grants. There are equipment grants, but these are different from trying to stock the storeroom. Contact the program officer about restraints and limits on equipment. Obviously, if it is a research grant and you need a mass spectrometer, go ahead, request it.

Principle 11. What are the cost-sharing requirements? Some agencies require from 5 to 100 percent in matching funds. Double check the guidelines. Can donated time be used as a match? Can newly purchased equipment be used? Must the match be cash? Find out before you prepare the proposal to save institutional embarrassment. A caution is needed here. If time is used, be certain that your time effort equals 100 percent, including the matching effort. Overtime is usually not allowed when time is used as a budgetary match. Time cost sharing must be documented by time certifications. Cost sharing should be kept to the minimum required by the guidelines. If there is no requirement in the guidelines, institutional research officers probably will not allow you to propose cost-share or matching. Cost sharing and matching (other than in-kind) are real (monetary) contributions or burdens on the institution and should be used wisely. Further, all nonfunded support, such as cost-sharing, matching, or in-kind support, create a significant administrative burden on both the principal investigator and central and unit administrators of the organization. If you do not meet your cost sharing commitment, the institution is in great jeopardy of losing the funding and experiencing further ramifications, such as institutional penalties or forfeiture of rights to propose future projects to some funding organizations. Cost sharing is a serious commitment and should be used prudently.

Principle 12. There is a termination date. Every grant has a beginning date when you may legally draw against the grant and a terminal, or closing, date. If, for any reason, you find you need more time but not more money to finish the project, request a "no cost extension" from your program officer. These requests must be made at least 60 days in advance of the termination date. Once the termination date has passed, if you do not have an extension, absolutely no additional funds may be charged against the project.

These 12 principles are enough for anyone. After all, Moses only received 10 commandments! Check your guidelines and if you have any budgetary questions, call the program officer and your finance officer for local policies. Those folks know what you are going through and they'll be most happy to provide suggestions.

Indirect Costs

Indirect costs are often called overhead or administrative costs. These are budgeted allocations made to grant recipient institutions by nearly all federal agencies and only a tiny number of foundations. Note how carefully that last point was stated, "to grant recipient institutions," not the project director. The indirect costs are added to the direct costs charged against a grant to conduct the actual project.

Examine the budget of the model grant proposal in Appendix B. You will observe the direct costs of salaries and wages, fringe benefits, supplies, travel, per diem, equipment or equipment rental, and contracts for services. Also included are the allowed participant costs of books, materials, travel, room and board, and stipends.

In this case, the institution was allowed a flat rate of eight percent for indirect cost recovery. These funds are given to the institution to defray such fixed costs as accounting, payroll, purchasing, administration, plant operations and maintenance, depreciation of buildings and equipment, and use of student services, such as admissions or registrar's offices. An institution or school district does not simply fix its own rate. The rates are established through a complex audit process that is described in OMB Circular A-21. Often the U.S. Department of Health and Human Services or the Department of Defense will establish a rate or, more usually, a series of rates that apply to different sectors or locations where the project takes place. For universities, these rates range from about 30 to 80 percent. Private contractors can go as high as 120 percent.

In the budget illustrated in Appendix B, the rate is a maximum of 8 percent, even though the institution's actual negotiated rate is 45 percent on-campus and 26 percent off-campus. The basic rationale and logic supporting indirect costs is that by contracting for selected services or products, it is more economical for the federal government to pay some administrative fee than it would be for the feds to build the laboratory, staff it, pay for its maintenance, and conduct the project.

Additionally, educational organizations have basic missions. When grants are awarded, the sponsored projects remove some space, time, equipment, and human resources from the institution's primary mission. Thus, the indirect cost rate is established to pay for costs not directly identified in the proposal but those indirectly benefiting the project. For example, some simple ones are local telephone calls, utilities for project offices, janitorial services, support to operate that mass spectrometer, safety services, and many other regular functions.

In research universities, it is easy to identify the hundreds of people employed due to the increased workload caused by awarded grants and contracts. Somebody has to do the paper work. How the indirect costs are spent or distributed is determined, in part, by OMB Circular A-21 and institutional policy. For example, enlightened administrators draft policies that allow some of the indirect costs to be returned to principal investigators as seed money for future activities. One university allocates 20 percent to departments and 10 percent to colleges. The remaining 70 percent is subdivided between actual operational costs, general fund obligations, international programs, research parks, employee benefits, carry-forward funds, and the graduate school.

In school districts, the amount is very small, usually 4 or 5 percent, but almost never exceeds an 8 or 10 percent maximum. At a major research university, a $1 million direct-cost grant could bring $450,000 or more to the indirect cost column. Don't worry, allowed indirect costs are a part of doing business and your proposal will not be rejected because of them alone. And, yes, federal auditors do review the annual indirect costs reported to the Feds (but seldom revealed to the public).

Other Budgeting Considerations _____

Cost-sharing was discussed in Principle 11. One great source of cost-sharing is to use the difference between the negotiated and actual indirect rate allowed by an agency. For example, in most cases the U.S. Department of Education allows eight percent maximum for indirect costs. Assume that your organization has an established rate of 50 percent. The cost-sharing is the difference, or 42 percent. If you received a $100,000 grant plus 8 percent for indirect costs, you use the difference, $42,000, as in-kind cost sharing. It's perfectly legitimate. A word of caution is needed, however, when making the calculations. If you use "indirect cost waivers," as it is officially called, the proposal budget justification must show a detail of the base. This specified base generally is the "total direct cost" and includes all direct costs except those specifically exempted within the guidelines. The "full" rates of most institutions are based on "modified total direct cost," containing a far more comprehensive list of direct-cost exclusions. Hence, in computing the indirect costs that have been waived, you must compute the full federally allowable indirect cost and subtract out the indirect cost allowable rather than applying a net rate. Discuss this method at great length with your own fiscal officer so that no errors are computed and the budget justification is clearly stated.

Disseminating results is also an allowable direct cost. This was mentioned in Principle 9. If you have a large developmental grant and you want to "get the word out to cosmopolites," a sizable amount of the direct costs could be allocated to this feature. During the curriculum development era of The National Science Foundation, the NSF, for five major projects, awarded $20.5 million for curriculum development costs and $22.9 million for implementation (dissemination) costs (Orlich 1987). Without implementation or dissemination activities, diffusion of ideas or products would be limited. Business calls these activities advertising. Participants can be paid an honorarium for attending workshops, institutes, or inservice programs. Again, the guidelines will provide details.

Just as the project gets underway, you discover that one line item has more than you need and another has much less. Now what? Call the program officer. Explain the situation. In nearly all reasonable cases, you will be allowed to make shifts between budget lines. Some agencies even allow you a 10 percent shift in any category without requesting permission. If a major change is required, you may have to submit a new budget for agency approval. In many instances, you'll be called by the program officer to cut the budget by some percentage. Be prepared with a contingency plan and a reduced scope of work.

The best way to learn about budgeting is to do one, although our model in Appendix B will give you a good idea how they are constructed. You must have your budget approved by your own institutional budget office prior to the full proposal's submission. To help you critique your fiscal plan, a budget checklist follows.

Budget Checklist
1. Budget lines coincide with narrative.
2. All budget activities are mentioned in the proposal.
3. Accurate data are presented.
4. Institutional policies guide specific allocations.
5. Uniform percentage changes are used for long-term budgets.
6. The guidelines are meticulously followed.
7. Any deviations are first approved by your program officer.
8. Your budget office approved the plan.
9. A reduced-scope contingency plan is established.

7
Preparing Research Proposals

AT LAST COUNT, THERE WERE MORE THAN $16,000$ BOOKS ADDRESSING research—its design, methods, and theory. The wealth of these resources makes it redundant for me to discuss all aspects of the topic here. Yet, a book on grant proposal writing would be criticized if research was not at least mentioned. Thus far, I discussed grant proposals from the perspective that research grants go to individuals or groups who have a fully established research program. Let us now examine the implications for "extramural" funding.

Research Programs

For most, the field of public education is cluttered with one-shot studies that neither lead to theory building nor hypothesis testing. The National Academy of Sciences criticized the trite and irrelevant studies that pass for research in education. This is no small indictment. Even Elliot W. Eisner, former president of the American Educational Research Association, wrote in 1984 that when doing research there was a tendency to "conduct educational commando raids to get the data and get out" (Eisner 1984, p. 451). Such short-duration projects will not be funded in major national competitions.

Following the general perspective of the scientific disciplines will resolve this condition. Well-funded scientific researchers all have long-term, well-established research programs or agendas. They don't chase dollars by skipping from one opportunistic topic or faddish issue to another—

at-risk kids, school reform, attention deficit disorders, outcome-based education. Unfortunately, this scenario is all too common in schools of education. Top scientific researchers establish programs based on tough problems that as yet have no reasonable descriptions or solutions. They carefully select significant problems. These problems are well supported by theory, or predictive and supportive hypotheses. Experiments are carefully designed. In most cases, research scientists spend one or two years working in postdoctoral fellowships. The research internship for these individuals is grueling.

Compare this with education. There is a tendency to complete the Ed.D. or Ph.D. with no extended work in a research laboratory or center. The bulk of Ed.D.'s are in reality part-time commuters teaching full-time. They conduct enough of a qualitative study (very much in vogue now) or some quantitative study to suffice their committees. In my 34 years of working full-time in higher education, I only met one colleague who had postdoctoral experience in education. Thus, the graduate training programs are client centered, not discipline centered as they are in the sciences.

Basic research is done in the sciences and not in education. After all, education is the engineering arm of the social sciences—it may be almost impossible to do pure and basic research in education. Yet, the applied studies are short-term and they need not be. There are, to be sure, several educational researchers who have distinguished careers in dealing with significant long-term applied studies. At the risk of offending some individuals, I will simply list a few areas where excellent long-term research has been published in education:

Class Size and Student Achievement
Cooperative Learning
Early Childhood Interventions
Individually Guided Instruction
Inquiry Teaching Models
Mastery Learning
Operant Conditioning
Questioning
Socioeconomic Impact on Learning
Tutorial Instruction

These topics have been studied by individuals, groups, and research and development centers. As a result, an emerging body of credible literature is available for making policy or instructional decisions based on data, not whims.

Successful research programs usually have long-range viability, because to obtain competitive funds at the national level investigators must be able to demonstrate some success. If you seek research grants from the National Institutes of Health (NIH) or the NSF, you must already have published successful studies. Research in this sector means publishing.

To begin a research program, obtain the small grants often offered as seed money in universities or forward-looking school districts. With these funds you begin a program, gain some success, chalk-up a few victories, establish a set of credible publications, and you are ready for the "big ones."

Testing Hypotheses

Successful research proposals incorporate all the elements previously discussed: problem, hypotheses, objectives, procedures where specific protocols are presented, subjects, personnel, equipment, travel, stipends, and indirect costs. Funded researchers carefully design their studies, but they always have specific objectives. More importantly, long-range research problems test hypotheses.

Research Hypotheses

A research hypothesis is a statement that may concern cause-and-effect relationships. Often it is written using the logic of the "if-then" syllogism. Scientific fields have literally thousands of research hypotheses. In the social-behavioral sciences, where education should be classified, the research hypothesis may not be as well specified. In most cases, few teachers actually can state a research hypothesis that may have been inferred from empirical studies. Hypotheses are only as good as their ability to predict the probability of future actions or consequences. That is why there are so few in education.

Null Hypotheses

To determine if a hypothesis is testable in statistical terms, it is usually stated in the null form. The null hypothesis is a statement that asserts that differences between groups will be due to chance, not the experimental statement.

"There will be no significant differences on [dependent variable] the Iowa Test of Basic Skills between students who learn [treatment] mathematics via computer-aided instruction and [control] those who learn via large group instruction."

This form of the null hypothesis means that no significant differences will be observed between post-test results of the two groups. If the data show no significant differences, then we "tentatively accept the research hypothesis." That is, there will be no statistical differences. If, however, one treatment group shows a statistical difference over the other group, then we "do not accept the null hypothesis." By not accepting the null hypothesis, the research hypothesis is accepted. Null hypotheses are usually stated in the objectives or purpose section of the proposal. One sequence of topics in a research grant proposal could be:

> Purpose of Study
> Statement of Objectives
> Research Hypothesis
> Null Hypothesis
> Level of Statistical Significance
> Review of Literature

The researcher selects the level of statistical significance at which the null hypothesis will not be accepted. If you were willing to accept results that could be due to chance alone five times out of 100, then the .05 level of statistical significance would be specified by the researcher. The level of statistical significance is established before the study is conducted, not after. We already discussed using effect size in Chapter 5. In many cases this is more meaningful than the tests of significance.

Refer to any of the standard textbooks on statistics or research for an elaboration of hypothesis testing. My intent is to present an introduction to the topic as it pertains to proposal writing so you may realize some of the details that affect the way you prepare a research proposal.

The educational relevance of the null hypothesis is, of course, another question. The field of educational research has some evidence to show the triviality of many proposed research or null hypotheses. Unfortunately, most education researchers do not adequately control their experiments to allow for a major generalization. The single criterion for a research hypothesis is whether it can be empirically tested. As in scientific research, the experiment may well be the best technique for settling educational arguments. Of course, these experiments must meet the rigors of accepted methodology. In education, the subjects are not as controllable as are physical objects, and thereby create "messy" conditions or less than desirable controls.

Various Methodologies—Nonexperimental Designs

There are several different methodologies that can accomplish a set of objectives. I will briefly expand on the following types:

Surveys
Curriculum Development Projects
Staff Development Projects
Case or Qualitative Studies
Experimental Designs

Surveys

A frequently used methodology in the field of education is the survey. Surveys are used to collect data about a specific trait or to obtain opinions concerning a set of concepts, ideas, or programs. The survey is basically comprised of: (1) a set of objectives; (2) instruments (e.g., questionnaires or personal interview schedules); and (3) a sample of respondents. The most important part of the survey is preparing the data collection instrument. To conduct longitudinal studies, you need some testable hypotheses.

The sample may be selected by polling the entire population (e.g., teachers in a state), or by choosing a nonbiased sample on a random basis. In some cases, a stratified random sample is chosen. The latter technique is used to ensure representation from various subgroups of the population. Whatever sampling plan is used, it should be written in detail identifying who will be sampled, how the sample was established, and why the techniques are being used.

Curriculum Development Projects

A commonly funded research activity often relates to the production of needed courses, units, or modules. Curriculum development goes beyond the mere formulation of a course of study. A curriculum study design is normally composed of a statement of objectives, description of methodology, scope and sequence of learning experiences, description of content, and specification of procedures for evaluating the effectiveness of the curriculum. Objectives should be stated concisely in terms of student learning and, perhaps, behaviors, and translated into criteria for evaluating the curriculum. Recent advances in subject matter and learning theory should be reviewed as needed. The proposal should stress investigative or experimental activities rather than program implementation. The project should be innovative for the investigator undertaking it and should hold promise for contributing to curriculum improvement in other settings (i.e., be transportable or generalizable).

Curriculum activities generally fall within the areas of development or validation, or a combination of the two. A small project might be designed to create or to validate selected curriculum materials or methods as part of a larger curriculum effort. In unusual cases, a study could meet the requirements of a total curriculum effort in a specifically limited curriculum area.

When research is primarily for developing curriculum, the proposal should do the following:

• Describe the theoretical background, related research, and bases by which new types of student experiences will relate to the objectives of instruction.

• Designate which curriculum design areas are involved and reflect knowledge of previous work in the area.

• Illustrate the process or procedure to be used, giving attention to how the present curriculum will be improved.

Curriculum development usually leads to producing a "product" at the completion of the project. The product may be a simulation, book, learning module, multimedia device, or set of methods for instruction. The procedures for curriculum development projects should specify the form of the final product. (Hint: In these projects, work with a publishing company as a cooperating partner. This assures dissemination.)

When the research is primarily validation of curriculum products or processes, the proposal should:

• Delineate the area of curriculum design under investigation.

• Identify the relevant variables designated for study and the procedures for determining the effects of these variables.

• Describe the population involved, the data to be gathered, and the instruments to be used.

The rationale for curriculum validation projects is to determine the appropriateness of curriculums in different environments. Usually, one desires to know if a curriculum will achieve its intended end with groups of students who were not involved in its initial development. As integrated curriculums become an accepted part of instruction, several validation studies will need to be conducted to determine the efficacy of the curriculum materials prior to large-scale adoptions. Such research will reduce the chances of the classic blunder of the Physical Science Study Committee (PSSC) that developed a rigorous high school physics curriculum in the early 1960s. The PSSC was designed for the very best high school students. Guess who was convinced to use it—all high school physics teachers. You didn't need the Enrico Fermi Prize to predict the almost total collapse of high school physics enrollments because of this type of product dissemination and lack of curriculum validation by a group who should have been more empirically oriented. If materials do not teach well or the students incur great learning difficulties, the materials simply are not working. (Of course, this assumes teacher behaviors appropriate to the curriculum and prerequisite learning skills by the students.) Curriculum validation projects are very essential to the success of the total school program—and to the success of the students.

Staff Development Projects

Staff development or inservice education is very much a part of research and development. This aspect might be one area that is underdeveloped. Regardless of what has been written about outcomes of school reform and a myriad of other educational techniques, in the last analysis innovations are implemented by the staff. An aware and sensitive staff is the basis for change. Preparing a staff development project is almost identical to preparing a curriculum project, except the emphasis is on preparing selected staff with a set of competencies, instructional methods, curriculum techniques, or program skills.

Case Studies

Social workers, counselors, teachers, administrators, and many others have long used case studies. The studies are an attempt to provide objective descriptions of what takes place (behaviors, conditions, attitudes) with usually no attempt to manipulate variables; medical case studies, of course, are an exception. Manipulating variables means that the independent variable is systematically applied to the subjects in question. Qualitative studies and action research studies are all very similar. (Purists will scorn me for such a cavalier treatment.)

These studies are helpful for fact finding and for describing changes that may take place in individuals, organizations, or instructional techniques. When using these methodologies, you must be cautious that personal bias or systematic observational bias is not inadvertently built into the design. These methods require a detailed examination of one subject, instruction, or community considered as a unit. Drawing inferences or conclusions from them requires a great deal of caution. Some researchers argue that no generalizations should be made. As grounded theory is generated, however, the statements may be converted into testable hypotheses. This genre of studies is most helpful in identifying possible leads that might isolate critical independent or dependent variables. The latter could then be tested through experimental studies.

Experimental Designs

The previous methodologies typically do not use control and experimental groups wherein the experimental group receives the manipulated or independent variable. In "true" experimental research, the independent variable must be carefully controlled and applied. To be certain that some outcome or trait is caused by the experimental treatment, large groups of subjects or students are needed. This section will not attempt to describe all experimental designs since there are many books on that topic. What will be presented are a few basic tenets of experimental design that can be used effectively by any researcher who desires to control or manipulate one independent variable or set of variables.

Typically, variables are classified as independent and dependent. The independent variable is some characteristic, behavior, procedure, or curriculum that ought to be associated with some effect or dependent variable. The classic experiment with Pavlov's dog might be called to mind. Remember, Pavlov rang a bell each time the dog was fed. Ultimately, Pavlov could ring the bell (independent variable) and the dog would salivate (dependent variable) without being fed. In all experimental designs, it is usually assumed that if some independent variable occurs, it will be associated with another characteristic or observable event—the dependent variable. Specified conditions are needed to produce such a relationship.

A few years ago, a study was conducted that concluded there was a somewhat high probability of a student's owning a car in high school and receiving relatively poor grades. The independent variable was owning a car, and the dependent variable was receiving relatively poor grades. To test this hypothesis, you could predict success in high school as measured by grades and automobile ownership. The only problem is that the correlation is so low that the predictions are no better than chance alone. Why the discrepancy? There are too many other independent variables associated with auto ownership and grades in high school. Further, correlations rarely, if ever, determine cause and effect.

As you plan for research experiments, consider the following factors:

Instrumentation (tests or measurement devices)
Subjects
Selection of control and experimental groups
Independent variable (the treatment)
Post-testing
Analysis of results

Instrumentation. Instruments that measure changes in behaviors must be developed early in any research design. If measures are not available (e.g., to measure the efficacy of teaching mathematics via computers or by large group instruction), then the investigator must design them. In such cases, parallel forms are usually needed for pre- and post-tests, as are determinations of instrument reliability and validity. Pre-testing is essential in establishing a baseline for comparing later results. In other words, you want to know where all subjects rank prior to administering any independent variable. If you find that some subjects already know what you will be teaching, then they must be screened out of the experiment since their scores will contaminate both pre- and post-test results.

If the subjects are truly randomly assigned to experimental and control groups, a pre-test is not always necessary because any differences between groups on the post-test will reflect changes produced by introducing the independent variable (i.e., the experimental treatment). Instruments may be adapted from those already published. If you adapt an instrument that has a copyright, however, be sure to seek written permission from the publisher before you alter it. If not, you may be the subject of litigation.

Where explicit outcomes are specified, criterion measures may be converted into the instruments and used collectively to form the standards for determining achievement. Regardless of the approach, reliable and valid tests should be used. The researcher ought to know for whom the tests were designed and how accurately they predict traits for the intended group.

Subjects. Subjects used in an experiment should have rather homogeneous selected traits. You need to be sure that all subjects exhibit approximately the same trait prior to applying the independent variable with the experimental group. If the sample of subjects is randomly selected and randomly assigned to the control and experimental groups, however, the variability of traits will probably not affect the outcome. By using randomization, the researcher will avoid inadvertently introduced bias. The results from replicated random group experiments are usually more generalizable than are those where extensive statistical manipulations must be performed to equalize the groups. Subjects must be selected without building in a bias that will favor your treatment group. For example, it would be very unfair to match 15-year-old boys against 15-year-old girls on some skill that requires physical strength; but one might match them on some manual dexterity program.

One last caution about the use of human subjects in experimental studies—according to federal regulations adopted by the U.S. Department of Health and Human Services, no human subject may be exposed to experimentation that could cause physical or psychological harm. Researchers who desire to study sensitive issues such as sexual habits, religion, family interactions, or personal habits may find their proposals flatly rejected.

Control and Experimental Groups. Once the sample of subjects is defined, they ought to be randomly assigned to the treatment groups. The control group has no independent variable administered, while the experimental group receives the independent variable. Students, or as they are called in design, "the subjects," should be randomly selected for groups. Random means exactly that. The most random method of selection is to place the names of all subjects in a hat, thoroughly mix them, and draw one name alternately for the control and experimental groups. If this is not possible, entire classes should be drawn from the hat to determine those that will act as experimental and those that will act as control. Teachers would also be assigned to those classes in the same random manner. Such a selection ensures the elimination of bias.

Independent Variable. The independent variable is administered to the experimental group. This is the group, for example, to receive instruction in math via computers, or whatever. The control group receives the same instruction with the exception of the independent variable treatment. This is difficult to achieve in the same school, since students frequently interact. Thus, there is a chance that your experimental group may exhibit the "Hawthorne Effect." This means that since they know they are subjects for an experiment, they might act differently than they normally would in the same situation. This effect is controlled by using randomly selected groups from different schools, or by giving the control group something different to do. In this manner, all groups will think they are doing something unique. The best method to counteract the Hawthorne Effect is not to tell any of the subjects that they are in some new program, or that they are in some experiment. Make it business as usual for all groups. It is essential that the researcher carefully control the independent variable treatment. This will lessen chances for contamination occurring in either group.

Post-testing. In some designs, there is only one pre-test and one post-test. This is very unfortunate since project success is contingent on only one student performance— the post-test. I would like to suggest that a series of performance checks be made throughout the duration of the experiment via formative evaluations, which are specifically designed to monitor the project. This means a systematic assessment or test at each phase of the experiment should be made. From the series of formative measures, data may be derived that can be compared to the baseline for all groups and for different time intervals. The post-test or summative test is the final testing of all groups. The post-test should be given at the same time to all groups to avoid contaminating the data.

Analysis of Results. Analyzing the data, test results, or comparisons between or among groups is essential. In most cases, parametric statistical tests will be used. These tests must be planned in advance so the collected data will meet the assumption of each specific statistical analysis. Many school districts have evaluation specialists. Identify these individuals before the project is funded so that data analysis may be conducted easily through electronic data processing equipment.

When designing the project, you should address the elements above. If your research yields interesting results, the test will probably be replicated or duplicated at other sites or your lab to determine the efficacy of the independent variable. That means no end to being a "grants junkie." This may all sound overpowering to the novice who has a good idea, but remember, ideas are not funded—*procedures* are. Collectively, the procedures, hypotheses, and objectives must support each other. This does not mean curbing your creativity. It simply means that you will logically and systematically develop your creative efforts so they may be funded.

Reviews and Certifications

You have just spent the past eight weeks crafting your research proposal. Three internal reviewers gave you great feedback and encouragement. Then, the director of research said, "Where are your certifications and assurances?" As Yogi Bera profoundly stated, "It ain't over 'til it's all over." What is left to do? Plenty.

At this writing there are 12 separate assurances or certificates that you prepare. The most critical is protecting human subjects. This will be expanded in the next section. Others concern these areas:

Treatment of vertebrate animals
Claim for inventions and patents
Freedom from previous debarment or suspension
Maintenance of a drug-free workplace
Disclaimer from lobbying
No delinquent federal debts (for you or your
    institution)
Policies regarding misconduct in science
Civil rights assurance
Nondiscrimination against disabled individuals
No sex discrimination
No age discrimination

Certificates for each of these must be prepared. Additionally, if your research uses radioactive materials, recombinant DNA, carcinogenic chemicals, or any hazardous items, special care must be noted in the proposal.

Human Subject Review

As you can quickly infer, these requirements came about over the past 25 years as unethical or fraudulent claims were made. Every time a researcher goes beyond the ethics or morals of the community, a new assurance is added. The most acclaimed example of unethical treatment of human subjects is, of course, the infamous Tuskegee case found to be a misguided syphilis study instituted by the U.S. Public Health Service in the 1930s. The news broke in July of 1972 that 600 black men had been involved in a 40-year nontreatment study—even though cures were available. Congress reacted quickly with passage of The National Research Act (PL 93-348), signed into law on July 12, 1974. The act established criteria for using human-related research.

Discussions and regulations on treatment of humans are voluminous. I will give just an orientation so you will be able to check with your Institutional Review Board (IRB). Every research university, institution, or hospital has an IRB. The board is charged to review all research proposals involving humans. A proposal will neither be sent for funding nor permitted to be done without funding if the IRB concludes that there are risks to the human subjects that outweigh the gains in knowledge. The risks may be physical, emotional, or psychological discomfort; stress; or invasion of privacy. Further, if sensitive issues are being addressed (e.g., sexual experiences, drug or alcohol use, or collection of data that may damage the subject's financial standing, employability, or reputation), then the researcher must describe the risks and how the risk will be handled or compensated. One key element is the "informed consent" certificate. All subjects must be told of potential risks and that a subject may withdraw from the study at any time without fear of reprisal.

For research projects where there is no or minimal risk, such as most training or curriculum development projects, the IRB review may be expedited. If you use a questionnaire, the IRB may examine only those questions that are considered sensitive. With self-administered questionnaires, the general reaction is implied consent. If the respondent sends back the completed questionnaire then that action is inferred as implied consent. You must not identify any respondent by name; that is considered an invasion of privacy.

Other Concerns

Depending on your own institutional policy, you might be asked to certify that certain conditions are or are not required. For example:

Ample space
Radiation safety
Security clearances
Special laboratory services
Commitment for matching funds
Regional clearinghouse approval
Conflict of interest
Outside contractors
Extra library support
Mainframe computer uses
Foreign travel

These 11 considerations are often required by the institution to protect itself. You can imagine a university president's surprise on learning that a $100,000 research grant was awarded to a professor at the school with the contingency that the school will construct a $2 million laboratory for conducting the study.

Much more could be added. The rationale for including this chapter was to identify some key elements of successful research proposals. To aid in your efforts, one more handy guide follows. Use it to evaluate your proposal before the final submission.

Detailed Evaluation Checklist for Research Proposals

NA = Not Applicable
1 = Very Inadequate
2 = Inadequate
3 = Adequate
4 = Very Adequate

Needs or Problem

Needs for project are clearly stated.   1 2 3 4

Needs for project are clearly documented.   1 2 3 4

Problem is significant.   1 2 3 4

Objectives

Objectives are clearly stated.   1 2 3 4

Objectives are related to identified needs.   1 2 3 4

Objectives are measurable or observable.   1 2 3 4

Procedures

Limitations of the project are stated.   NA 1 2 3 4

Important terms are defined.   NA 1 2 3 4

Procedures to conduct project are
described explicitly.   1 2 3 4

Procedural design is appropriate to
accomplish objectives.   1 2 3 4

Procedures are appropriately sequenced.   1 2 3 4

Population of study is described.   NA 1 2 3 4

Method of identifying population is
appropriate.   NA 1 2 3 4

Data-gathering methods or procedures
are described.   NA 1 2 3 4

Data-gathering methods or procedures
are appropriate.   NA 1 2 3 4

Review of literature is appropriate.   NA 1 2 3 4

Evaluation

Evaluation design or data analysis is
specified.   NA 1 2 3 4

Evaluation is oriented toward project
objectives.   NA 1 2 3 4

Assurances

Human subject assurances are clearly identified.	NA	1	2	3	4
Animal care is specified.	NA	1	2	3	4
Any hazard is clearly discussed.	NA	1	2	3	4
Consent form is appended.	NA	1	2	3	4
Expedited IRB approval.	NA	1	2	3	4

General

Budget is adequate or realistic to conduct project.	1	2	3	4
Proposal is explicitly written.	1	2	3	4
Proposal is logically organized.	1	2	3	4
Proposal displays unbiased style.	1	2	3	4
Project is transportable or results publishable.	1	2	3	4
Project is socially or educationally significant.	1	2	3	4
The proposal was internally reviewed.	1	2	3	4

The probability for funding the proposal as now written is:

8
Submitting the Proposal

WHAT A GREAT FEELING—JOY AND RELIEF. THE FINAL DRAFT OF THE proposal is complete. But it's still too soon to celebrate. There are some necessary details that you must attend to. Let's examine how the very successful grant swingers complete the process.

Planning for Details

First, compare the entire proposal against the guidelines. Examine each criterion and subcriterion. Did you address every item? If not, then make the addition right now. Keep in mind that the reviewers of your proposal will be given evaluation checklists similar to those illustrated in the book passim. Each criterion will be weighted with a set number of points, (e.g., Needs-10 points, Plan of Operation-40 points). To be successful, you must get as many points as possible. That is why you double check every section in the guidelines or evaluation criteria if you have them.

Next, review your headings. Do you use the same words as the guidelines? If not, go back and change them. For example, if the guidelines call the initial section "Significance of Project" and you have it labeled "Introduction" then some reviewers will miss that whole area and deduct all the points from your proposal because you did not specifically type out the words "Significance of Project." Double check all the headings in your proposal so they are identical to those used in the guidelines. Remember, you're seeking funding, not creative synonyms. Check for parallel construction. When you made lists, did you use the same grammatical construction? That means using all infinitives or all gerunds when listing items. Refer to Chapter 4 where the lists of objectives are shown. Note how each list is parallel. Parallel lists aid the reviewer and reduce confusion.

Sure you spell-checked your document on computer, but have you carefully read the entire paper? Often, at this stage of the writing process, it is better to ask someone else to proof because you are too close to it to catch the errors. In the final typing of the manuscript, did you meet or exceed the page limitation? If you exceeded it, go back and edit, reducing some sections. Foundations and agencies really mean it when they specify rigid page limitations. I know a colleague who did not believe in following this criterion. His entire set of proposals was returned with a little preprinted card informing him that his page counts exceeded the specified limit. It was very embarrassing.

If you need your proposal package postmarked by a certain day, and you're down to that day, send the package via certified mail, receipt return. Certified mail is your only guarantee that the postmark is valid. Sorry, your school's Pitney-Bowes mailing system is not acceptable—it is too easy to back date. Don't take any chances with the postmark. Spend a few extra dollars from your own hard-earned money and send it certified, receipt return via the U.S. Postal Service.

If you must get the package to its proper destination by a set deadline day and hour, then plan ahead. I always give myself a two-day leeway just in case a storm closes the airport for 24 hours at the central collection point for one of our express service companies or overnight mail. Don't race to the deadline, allow some slack.

Who had to sign the official cover sheet? If someone else must sign, be sure to notify that person's office and alert the person that you need a signature. Use the same action when collecting letters of endorsement. I work with school districts. In nearly all of my grant applications, a superintendent or a representative of a group of superintendents sends us a letter of endorsement. Be certain to have that original well in hand before a crisis of hours appears. Further, as was mentioned earlier, if you need a school board's approval, or some agency approval, find out when they meet. You need to make a series of timelines or a master PERT chart to plan the needed actions prior to submitting the proposal on time.

Did you have at least two or three colleagues internally review the proposal? You must. I can honestly say that when we have done that, we bat almost 1.000. When we do not, for some reason, the average drops to 0.400. Yes, internal reviewers find areas of concern or weakness. You have time to modify the proposal before it is sent out. Don't wait for the external panel to notify you of weaknesses. Or, as I like to tell my colleagues, "I don't wear my feelings on my shirt sleeves." Their feedback is critical.

In Chapter 7, I noted that 12 or more assurances or certifications must be made, depending on the nature of the proposal. You may not have to certify against halitosis or dandruff, but there will be at least nine different assurances that will be submitted when you seek federal funding. Be certain to have these items of "red tape" accomplished early. You don't want to miss a deadline because the civil rights assurance is missing. Perhaps the title of this chapter should be "plan, plan, plan." You must plan for all final activities related to the proposal.

Well, you have been diligent, planned well ahead, and completed all the little detail busters previously described. The proposal is copacetic; now just one little detail remains. Since you have to send 13 copies unsigned and two copies signed, and you are ready to take this stack to your official sending group, do one last check. Physically examine each proposal to count pages. Yes, you have a whiz-bang photocopy machine. But machines do make mistakes, one of the common ones being not duplicating page 12 or running page 14 twice. This is the final checkpoint. Examine each proposal to make certain that no page is missing. I sat on an NSF panel where such an incident occurred. The results were no funding. How could the panel complete its review? Two pages were missing. Zero points were allocated for that section. Sorry.

Why Are Proposals Rejected?

From time to time, you will have a proposal that does not get funded. In that case, call or write the program officer and request the comments made by the review panel. Private foundations will not react to your request, but public agencies must. Examine the panel's comments so you can understand why you received the letter of declination.

Over the years, personnel in The National Science Foundation have observed weaknesses that are common to nonfunded proposals. Sometimes a good proposal is not funded due to a lack of available funds. The NSF list in Figure 8.1 is constructed with the key point to the left and the critical elements to the right. After you check these 22 items, you should have a better understanding of the entire review process. Some of the suggestions listed in Figure 8.1 address major weaknesses, while others address ways to avoid relatively minor weaknesses. Remember, however, that the cumulative effect of minor problems can still result in a proposal's denial.

The Review Process

Your proposal has safely and in a timely manner found its way to the correct location for review. How does that process function? Depending on the agency or foundation, it generally works like this:

The proposal is logged-in and you receive a card with a control number. A program officer will read the proposal and complete an evaluation form. Next, one of several techniques will be used. The proposal may be mailed to external reviewers who read and evaluate it individually. Their scores are tallied by the program officer and when all data are in, the proposals are rank-ordered, and the top ones funded. A second common technique is to assemble a review panel at some city or agency. They critique each proposal individually and then discuss the merits of each collectively. A third technique is a combination of the first two. A fourth technique is to assemble two independent panels. Each panel is given, say, the same 10 proposals to review. Panel One is required to read and review them in order 1, 2, 3 . . . 10. Panel Two is instructed to read and review the proposals in the order 10, 9, 8, . . . 1. This method attempts to reduce panel bias and fatigue factors.

Figure 8.1
Reasons for Proposals Being Rejected

GENERAL

Follow Guidelines

1. Generally, the weaknesses of most proposals can be corrected by careful adherence to the guidelines.

Involve Others

2. The strongest proposals appear to be those in which the improvement plans are based on a prior assessment of institutional needs and have been carefully developed by the faculty. In these proposals, comprehensive plans and activities are set forth rather than a simple listing of needs by individual units.

NARRATIVE

Provide Rationale

3. Provide adequate information within the narrative on the proposed plan, including evidence of a needs assessment, rationale for the proposed approach, and evidence that the approach will work at the particular institution.

State Objectives and Activities Clearly; Tie to Budget

4. Clearly state project objectives and tie these to specific activities. Make clear the relationship between the proposed activities and the budget. Provide discussion within the narrative of all activities for which budget requests are made and include within the budget request those activities discussed in the narrative that are proposed for support.

Request Eligible Activities Only

5. Request support only for eligible activities and disciplines. Examples of ineligible activities are remedial courses and those based upon increased enrollment. Ineligible fields for the NSF include history, business, education, reading, and clinically-oriented activities.

(continued)

Figure 8.1 *(continued)*
Reasons for Proposals Being Rejected

Relevant Skills of Project Director	6. Give careful thought to project personnel. This is especially true for the director who should be selected on the basis of technical and administrative skills relevant to the project. Additionally, key project personnel must have sufficient time available to carry out project activities. Curriculum vitae should be provided for the proposed project director as well as for other key faculty and consultants.
Relevant Faculty Skills	7. Present clear evidence of existing faculty expertise in a particular strategy proposed in the project. Evidence of faculty computer experience should be presented if major computer equipment purchases have been requested in the proposal.
Timetable	8. Carefully consider the timing of activities; identify major milestones and establish a timetable for initiation and completion of these.
Describe Existing Programs	9. Describe the existing program, including faculty and facilities.
Relate to Institutional Goals	10. Indicate how the proposed plan fits into the institution's own goals or mission.
Evaluation Plan	11. Provide an adequate plan for evaluation of the project, including provision for collecting baseline data and other record keeping related to determining project impact.
Continuation Plan	12. Include a plan for continuation of project activities.
Endorsement of Central Administration	13. Be certain that the local review statement is specific and that it outlines the administration's commitment (philosophical and financial) to continuing of project activities.
Follow Guidelines	14. Stay within page limits specified in the guide and follow the format outlined in the guide.

(continued)

Figure 8.1 *(continued)*
Reasons for Proposals Being Rejected

BUDGET

Explain Budget and Provide	15. Provide a clear and detailed explanation of the proposed budget.
Justification	16. Provide justification for the proposed budget items.
List Equipment	17. List proposed equipment, materials, and supplies, in detail. This is especially important for equipment items costing more than $1,000. Equipment certification must be provided for special purpose equipment costing more than $10,000. Provide a list of existing major equipment holdings in areas involved in the project.
Indirect Cost Rate	18. Provide an up-to-date indirect cost rate for the institution. If the institution does not have an approved rate or the writer is a first-time applicant, the business officer should contact the Foundation's Division of Grants and contracts, Policy and Cost Analysis Branch.
Role of Consultants	19. Provide information on consultants—rate of payment, extent of involvement, curriculum vitae, exact role in the project. Note that local rates are to be used and that they cannot exceed daily rate of GS-18.
Observe Limitations	20. Make sure that requests do not exceed the established maximums for dollars and duration. Requests for shorter periods of time should be proportionately reduced. Budget requests which are out of line with stated limits often affect the way in which reviewers react to a proposal.
Proof	21. Carefully proofread the proposal for grammatical, spelling, and typographical errors. Such errors tend to give reviewers a poor impression of the proposal.
Request Comments	22. If denied, request comments and use them in resubmission.

Some readers start out tough and get easier as the day progresses. Other panel members are just the opposite. By having independent panels read proposals in reverse order, these two common biases tend to be canceled.

How do you get on a panel? Write a letter to the specific program officer requesting that your name be added to the lists. Usually, you will be sent a short form that you complete and return. Being a member of a panel is a great way to learn about crafting proposals. You'll wonder why some were submitted and you'll marvel at the best written ones. It is a must experience and it is professionally rewarding.

Wow, what could possibly be left? Plenty, but this is enough for a primer on crafting quality proposals, however, I could not close without another checklist. The final one illustrates a technical review form that will help you sharpen any reasonably prepared proposal. Good luck and much success in your proposal efforts. And don't forget to send a note of thanks to the program officer when you receive the letter that begins, "We are pleased. . . ."

Proposal Checklist for Technical Aspects

NA = Not Applicable
U = Unsatisfactory—needs major rewriting or revising.
S = Satisfactory—could use selected or minor improvement.
E = Excellent—AOK as written

General Construction

Opening statement		U S E
Lead-ins		U S E
Transitions between paragraphs		U S E
Closing		U S E
"V" development		U S E

Coherency

Syntax		U S E
Agreement (tense or number)		U S E
Logical consistency		U S E
Parallel construction		U S E

Clarity

Written explicitly		U S E
Appropriate word selection		U S E
No clichés		U S E
Terms are defined	NA	U S E

Organization and Format

Headings parallel guidelines		U S E
Consistency of tense		U S E
Correct form for long quotes	NA	U S E
Correct form for short quotes	NA	U S E
All quotes led in or out	NA	U S E
Citations	NA	U S E
Tables	NA	U S E
Figures	NA	U S E
Spelling/proofing		U S E
Overall Technical Evaluation		U S E

Qualitative Criteria

Development of ideas		U S E
Appropriate use of evidence		U S E
Data are relevant		U S E
Consistent with evaluative criteria		U S E
Originality/creativity		U S E
Overall Qualitative Education		U S E

Appendix A
Basic "Toolbox" for
Grant Seekers

Basic Tools to Connect with the Feds

Catalog of Federal Domestic Assistance. Superintendent
of Documents, P.O. Box 371954, Pittsburgh, PA 15250-7954.
($53)
Published annually, the CFDA contains descriptions of all
federal programs, including information on authorizing
legislation, purposes, eligibility, appropriations, information
contacts, application and award processes, and related
programs. The CFDA assigns numbers to each program. An
absolute must-have tool.

Commerce Business Daily. Superintendent of Documents,
Washington, DC 20402-9371. ($324 per year)
The CBD daily releases virtually all federal government
requests for bids, services, and buildings. This is for
professionals only; amateurs can't compete.

Commerce Business Daily Weekly Release. United
Communications Group, 11300 Rockville Pike, Suite 1100,
Rockville, MD 20852-3030. ($257 per year)
The weekly release is a customized report of the CBD for
those who do not desire the full daily set of notices. You
can contract for the specific codes desired.

Federal Register. Office of the Federal Register, National
Archives and Records Service, General Services
Administration, Washington, DC 20408. It may be ordered
from: New Orders, Superintendent of Documents, P.O. Box
371954, Pittsburgh, PA 15250-7954. A quicker way to obtain

individual copies is to write or call your closest United States Government bookstore. ($544 per year or $8 per single issue, Visa or Mastercard accepted)
The FR contains program regulations (proposed and final), announcements of deadlines, and funding criteria. This is a must for the individual, group, or institution desirous of seeking federal funds.

Large Tools to Tap Private Foundations

Annual Register of Grant Support: A Directory of Funding Sources. 28th edition (1995). R.R. Bowker, 121 Chanlon Road, New Providence, NJ 07974. ($189)
The 28th edition of the *Annual Register* provides information on 3,155 North American grant-making groups. Included are foundations, businesses, unions, governmental agencies, professional associations, and others. An excellent first source to initiate contact with potential funders.

Directory of Building and Equipment Grants. 3rd edition (1994). Richard M. Eckstein, ed., Research Grant Guides, Inc., P.O. Box 1214, Loxahatchee, FL 33470. ($57.50)
The editor identifies 948 foundations plus pages of federal agencies that can help you pinpoint funding for buildings or renovating them. Equipment grants are also identified.

Directory of Computer and High Technology Grants. 2nd edition (1994). Richard M. Eckstein, ed., Research Grant Guides, Inc., P.O. Box 1214, Loxahatchee, FL 33470. ($52.50)
If you are seeking funding sources for computers, software, or high-tech equipment, then this is a must. A total of 617 known funders are identified, plus 94 pages of federal agencies. This tool will easily be on the best-seller list.

Directory of Grants for Organizations Serving People with Disabilities. 8th edition (1993). Richard M. Eckstein, ed., Research Grant Guides, Inc., P.O. Box 1214, Loxahatchee, FL 33470. ($47.50)
The *Directory* lists 1,015 foundations, plus 55 pages of federal agencies that provide funding to improve the lives or environments of the disabled. An excellent starting reference.

The Foundation Directory 1995 Edition. 17th edition
(1995). Margaret Mary Feczko, ed., The Foundation Center,
79 Fifth Avenue, N.Y., NY 10003-3076. ($195)
The Foundation Directory is a great resource concerning the
largest grant-making foundations in the United States. Each
listed group has at least $2 million in assets and awards
$200,000 yearly. A total of 7,293 entries are listed. Another
good index to pinpoint funders, especially at local or state
levels.

The Foundation Directory, Part 2. (1995). Margaret Mary
Feczko, ed., The Foundation Center, 79 Fifth Avenue, N.Y.,
NY 10003-3076. ($175)
Part 2 describes foundations making annual awards
between $50,000 and $199,000 each year and having assets
of less than $2 million. Entries for 4,273 foundations are
included. Of interest to grant seekers, over 83 percent of
the donors specify some geographic limitation. This source
is a good starter.

The Foundation Grants Index 1995. 23rd edition (1994).
Ruth Kovacs, ed., The Foundation Center, 79 Fifth Avenue,
N.Y., NY 10003-3076. ($150)
Grants Index summarizes over 68,000 grants of at least
$10,000. Grants awarded by foundations or corporations
under that amount are excluded. This resource provides a
comprehensive list of who got funded and by whom. By
checking this source, you will know if you have a chance
with more than 1,000 different funders.

The Foundation 1000. (1995). Francine Jones, ed., The
Foundation Center, 79 Fifth Avenue, N.Y., NY 10003-3076.
($265)
The Foundation 1000 profiles 1,000 of the largest
foundations in the United States. The listed foundations
contribute about 65 percent of the yearly philanthropy.
Until 1992, the index was titled *Source Book Profiles*. Start
here for major foundations, contacts, addresses, financial
data, purposes, policies, and guideline information. Detailed
summaries of past funding initiatives are provided.

Foundation Grants to Individuals. 9th edition (1995). L.
Victoria Hall, ed., The Foundation Center, 79 Fifth Avenue,
N.Y., NY 10003-3076. ($55)

Here is one of the few guides that identifies 2,658 grants, scholarships, awards, or honors for the individual. You do not need an IRS 501 (c)(3) designation for most of the grants.

Guide of U.S. Foundations, Their Trustees, Officers, and Donors. Volume One (1995 edition). C. Edward Murphy, ed., The Foundation Center, 79 Fifth Avenue, N.Y., NY 10003-3076. ($225)
The *Guide* has 37,211 entries, including 33,983 foundations—private, corporate, or other. It also provides information on 3,729 foundations that give only to specified beneficiaries. If it exists in the United States, it will be listed in the guide. A great starter reference. Additionally, the *Guide* compiles a bibliography of all the state and local foundations directories by state. This resource is most valuable.

Guide to Funding for International and Foreign Programs. 2nd edition (1994). Margaret Mary Feczko, Ruth Kovacs, and Carlotta Mills, eds., The Foundation Center, 79 Fifth Avenue, N.Y., NY 10003-3076. ($85)
Here is a listing of 657 potential funders for grant seekers trying to locate foundations or corporate support for international programs. Statements of purpose, interests, and types of funding are included with each entry.

Guide to U.S. Foundations, Their Trustees, Officers and Donors. Volume Two, Indexes (1995 edition). C. Edward Murphy, ed., The Foundation Center, 79 Fifth Avenue, N.Y., NY 10003-3076. ($125)
The *Indexes* is a detailed compendium of all foundation trustees, officers, and donors in the United States. This index lists persons associated with large and small foundations. Each name is then keyed to a directory published by The Foundation Center. Here is a source to identify the affiliations of wealthy individuals.

National Directory of Corporate Giving: A Guide to Corporate Giving Programs and Corporate Funding. 3rd edition (1993). Carlotta R. Mills, ed., The Foundation Center, 79 Fifth Avenue, N.Y., NY 10003-0376. ($195)
Profiled are 2,050 companies that regularly make contributions to nonprofit groups. This directory is a

starting point when considering the solicitation of private sector funding. Further, the book has an extensive bibliographic listing of published papers about corporate funding.

Helpful Tools By Subscription

The Chronicle of Philanthropy. The Chronicle of Higher Education, P.O. Box 1839, Marion, OH 43306-2089. ($67.50/yr.)
The Chronicle of Philanthropy is a biweekly newspaper with a format similar to *The Chronicle of Higher Education.* The emphasis is on foundation and private sector giving. Awards, information, job availability, resources, current trends and much more are included in each issue, which averages about 64 pages with multipage supplements often inserted. For foundation watchers, this is an essential tool.

Education Grants Alert. Capitol Publications, Inc., P.O. Box 1453, Alexandria, VA 22313- 2053. ($299/yr.)
The Alert is published 50 weeks a year and offers subscribers a 100 percent money-back guarantee. Each issue highlights currently announced funding opportunities. Governmental and private competitions are covered in detail. Each issue also contains a page of tips that can help you prepare more effective proposals. Six areas are covered for each announcement: scope, deadline, funds, eligibility, areas, contact. This is a most helpful resource and is very timely; some issues arrive only three days following an *FR* announcement.

Foundation News. Council of Foundations, Inc., 1828 L Street, N.W., Washington, DC 20077- 6013. ($29.50/yr.)
Here is a bimonthly magazine that discusses the activities of various foundations. The funding priorities and changes of foundation personnel are presented in detail. If your organization will seek foundation support, the *News* can be an important addition to the library. This was formerly called *The Journal of Philanthropy.*

Other Tools for Writing Effective Proposals

The "How To" Grants Manual. 2nd edition (1993). David G. Bauer, The Oryx Press, 4041 North Central at Indian School Road, Phoenix, AZ 85012-3397. ($27.95)
David G. Bauer is a premier grant proposal writer and has authored other books and a series of 10 videotapes on the topic. His book provides ideas for planning, organizing, writing, and monitoring proposals.

Finding Funding: Grant Writing for the Financially Challenged Educator. (1993). Ernest W. Brewer, Charles M. Achilles, and Jay R. Fuhriman, Corwin Press, Thousand Oaks, CA. ($39.95)
Here is a book that virtually photocopies the *Catalog of Federal Domestic Assistance* and sections of the *Federal Register* to illustrate their uses. The authors show how to develop a competitive proposal.

Getting Funded: A Complete Guide to Proposal Writing. 3rd Edition (1988). Mary K. Hall, Portland State University Continuing Education Publications, P.O. Box 1491, Portland, OR 97207. ($19.95)
Mary K. Hall is an educator and former president of the Weyerhauser Company Foundation. Her guide gives a step-by-step approach to proposal writing. Included are scores of actual forms used by agencies.

Grant Application Writer's Handbook. (1995). Liane Reif-Lehrer, Jones and Bartlett Publishers, One Exeter Place, Boston, MA 02116. ($34.95)
This is a compendium for scientists who are seeking NIH funding. The author covers all details from idea generation to renewing an application. There are 100 pages of resources listed in one appendix and several sections represented from funded NIH and NSF grant proposals.

NB: All prices listed are subject to change.

Appendix B
Model of a Funded
Proposal

I<small>N THIS COPY OF A FUNDED PROPOSAL, LOCALES AND THE NAMES OF</small> individuals have been changed; everything else is verbatim. The budget that follows has been deliberately left open-ended so that you can fill in data and gain practice. If the data were given, you would not actively participate. To save space, two-page vitae of the personnel are excluded as are the letters of endorsement and various assurances. The 11 headings in the proposal are quoted directly from the guidelines.

North State Rural Science Project

1. Proposal Summary

This project is designed to meet the expressed science education needs of the K-12 state science teachers in the North Service Area. These needs have been documented to be a top priority and confirmed by the September 1993 North Science Conference and 1994 intensive review and critique. The goal is to develop science teachers who will provide district leadership for systemic changes in science curriculum and instructional strategies.

The objectives of the project are to: (1) provide selected science teachers with an understanding of the constructivist model of teaching science; (2) model an integrated science, technology, and societal program for teachers to use in their classrooms; (3) establish a support network of constructivist-oriented science teachers who model constructivist principles; and (4) implement strategies that encourage minorities, especially Native

Americans, Hispanics, and women to continue the study of science.

A one-week, intensive workshop will be held in Redding for selected science and technology teachers where participants will develop and prepare constructivist lessons for their students.

2. State Priority Addressed

The state priorities are those of: (1) developing competency for teachers in the use of instructional technology within the areas of science and mathematics at the middle level, (2) developing competency in mathematics and science for teachers assigned to teach these subjects at the secondary level, and (3) developing strategies for improving the access to instruction for historically underserved populations.

3. Program Audience and Development

This project is the product of a planning and writing team from (1) representative teachers of the area, (2) staff of the selected school districts, and (3) North State University faculty. At NSU, the Science Improvement Center (SIC) initially conducted an extensive needs assessment during the 1993-94 school year. The assessment indicated a need for additional training at the middle and secondary levels to augment the training delivered by NSU the last two years at the elementary level. Participants indicated a need to: (1) develop a constructivist approach in teaching at all levels for all children, (2) integrate up-to-date instructional technology into the pedagogy, and (3) establish a regional network for the rural schools for a support base.
A broad-based advisory team representing the area was formed to develop this project. Team members included Bill Jackson, Superintendent of Paradise Schools; Jane Perez, Assistant Superintendent Redding Schools; Fred Daniels, Superintendent of Red Bluff Schools; and Cedric Brown, Superintendent of Willows Schools.

Teachers who participated were Ray Fitzpatrick, Colusa; Victor Peterson, Red Bluff; Vicky Kingsley, Willows; Sam Johnson, Yuba City; Lance Rodgers, Live Oak; Mike Wilson, Upper Lake; and Patty Renz, Redding. They collaborated with the team led by Harvey Chandler,

Director of SIC and Charles Judd, Professor of Science Instruction from NSU. This proposal was jointly written by the above persons. Private school teachers will be invited to the workshop, and they have a history of high participation in NSU projects.

This project addresses both the needs of the under-represented minorities (i.e., women, Hispanics, and Native Americans), and regular students. Hispanics constitute a growing population in school districts in this area and Native American children are also widely distributed. The minority population is rapidly expanding in most districts.

Middle and secondary science teachers provide the leadership in science to rural school districts that have few resource or support specialists. Many times the teacher serves science needs through a wide grade-level range. Therefore, it is essential that these teachers have an opportunity to practice instructional strategies necessary for systemic change in the science curriculum in their districts.

Between 1991-1995, NASA grants to NSU have supported training for elementary teachers to become resources for their staffs in this geographical area. They do, however, look to the science content specialist for help and guidance. This proposal builds a leadership cadre of middle and secondary science teachers.

4. **Program Goals**

The primary goal of this project is to develop a leadership cadre of middle and secondary science teachers with an understanding of the constructivist model of teaching science.

The second goal is to infuse strategies to enhance science teaching with women and minorities as a part of this project.

These goals will be accomplished by the following objectives:

(1) Selected science topics will be explored with teachers in physical, biological, and earth sciences.

Laboratory activities will be organized relating to concepts of water quality, geology, environmental science, and health. The concepts associated with water quality will be carefully selected to expand each teacher's background for the appropriate sciences being taught in the respective grade levels. All participants will be provided with common experiences in conducting water quality studies in the area. Thus, the content will be relevant to each participant in his or her respective program.

(2) Selected topics which parallel objective one will be organized as a model for participants to integrate appropriate technology with mathematics, technology, and societal issues that relate to the theme of water quality.

Materials will be provided so that teachers may observe models of curriculum integration. The use of technology will be illustrated as a platform by which technology becomes an integral part of planning and teaching. The Science-Technology-Society (STS) model will be exemplified through a common water quality experience.

(3) Illustrative science materials for women, Hispanic, and Native American pupils will be featured.

Specific sets of materials will be provided so that the teachers can construct specific lessons that can be integrated into each teacher's science program.

(4) Peer support groups will be established to provide coaching on "process" skills, for example, thinking skills, questioning techniques, small group work and program evaluation.

Small groups of participants will be organized into support teams by school so that the interactive processes so essential to teaching constructivist-oriented science may take place. During the workshop, experiences will be provided and modeled for guided inductive and unguided inductive inquiry by using water quality research as the common theme. These two elements form the bases for the programs being reviewed as exemplars and are components of constructivist science teaching.

The above goals and objectives relate directly to the state priorities of providing greater access to science for underrepresented and underserved students. Minority teachers will be personally invited to attend the workshop by designated school district liaisons.

The above illustrates a model that utilizes local resource persons and builds a cadre network of teachers who are in close proximity.

Significance. This project has great significance in that it is the first time that a model created in one Eisenhower project is being disseminated and field-tested in a different context and geographic setting. This inservice mechanism uses intensive training with some follow-up activities that help to keep the network established.

The theoretical basis and original model are described at the end of the next section titled "Research Basis."

5. **Program Activities**

Workshop. A one-week, two-phase workshop will be conducted in June 1995, following school dismissal. The tentative dates are June 26-30th, 1995. Ten specific points will be incorporated into the workshop design.

Integrated concepts and processes
Teacher materials
Student materials
Constructivist model
National standards/America and Goals 2000
Instructional strategies
Evaluation
Special needs
Electronic networking, for example, e-mail, electronic bulletin boards
Cooperative research teams

During all sessions, the participants will always be involved with direct experiences with science materials needed to determine water quality—the theme being used as an exemplar. Integrated in the instruction will be instructing minority and disabled pupils so that science can be meaningful to them.

The evening format (Monday through Thursday) will be from 7 to 9 p.m. Three distinct aspects will be:

Cooperative research teams to share data
Development of pilot models for use "back home"
Networking among the selected schools

Water sampling sites will be selected along rivers, for example, Mill and Stony, and from local area ponds. During 1995-96, students will also test deep well samples. As data are collected, students will use mathematics and statistical analyses to compile a longitudinal record of activities. These data will be released to local media on a bimonthly basis.

We will also use teacher resource persons to help with the academic year inservice component. This will entail providing instruction to other teachers who were unable to attend the summer phase. Tentatively, they are Lance Rodgers, Live Oak; and Betty McDonald, Colusa. At least two follow-up, problem-solving meetings are planned for academic year 1995-96. Follow-up session number one will be held in conjunction with the annual regional science conference, to be held in Chico, November 3-4, 1995. Follow-up session number two will be held in Redding. During these sessions, we will meet to discuss the implementation of the project. During the fall conference, we will also present an orientation about the program for others.

Figure B-1 shows the program's activities.

Research Basis: Lev Vygotsky (1962) appears to be the founder of the constructivist philosophy of teaching and learning. This model requires a strong interaction between the presented material and the learner's personal thought processes and interactions. A major conclusion of Anne Batey and Sylvia Hart-Landsberg (1993) was that rural science teachers strongly endorsed the use of multiple senses that created an emotional engagement by which to create contextual memories. The latter implies that, in an intensive workshop, teachers will "learn" more and that they have a high probability of teaching as they were taught.

Again, the Batey and Hart-Landsberg classic, *Riding the Wind*, emphasizes the importance of direct access to materials to stimulate science aptitudes. Their report is most relevant as all participants in the project were from rural schools of the area.

Howard Gardner's (1983) seven forms of human intelligence shows that activities must facilitate the solving of problems or the creation of specific products. Thus, teachers and students need to be given opportunities to think in different ways. This project does that with the broad array of activities, built-in personal exchanges, and multimethodologies.

P. Cobb, E. Yackel, and T. Wood (1992) also noted that

Figure B-1
Immersion Model Schedule

	Monday
8 a.m. to Noon	Project Start-up: Define Problem, Form Research Groups
	Water Quality Data Gathering
	Tuesday
	Data Collecting of Water Quality on Site
	Wednesday
	Watershed Management Data Gathering on Site
	Thursday
	Develop Curricular Model for Districts
	Use of Technology
	Input Data into Regional Data Bank
	Friday
	Critique of Curriculum Models
	Integration of Technology
12 to 1 p.m.	LUNCH
1 p.m. to 5 p.m.	Monday
	Work with Cadre to Determine Water Characteristics on Site
	Preparing of Data Reports by Research Teams
	Tuesday
	Analyzing Data Laboratory
	Wednesday
	Modeling of Constructivist Principles
	Women and Minorities Workshop
	Thursday
	Curriculum Development
	Essentials for Gifted
	Friday
	Evaluation Models
	Plans for 1995-96 AY
	Completion
5 p.m. to 7 p.m.	DINNER
7 p.m. to 9 p.m.	Monday
	U.S. Army Corps of Engineers
	Tuesday
	Teachers Working with Actual Research Teams
	Wednesday
	"SITE" Network Design
	Thursday
	Network Building
	Use of Technology

effective constructivist learning models require that students be encouraged to ask questions. Therefore, it is critically important that teachers do not use questioning as a way to belittle students. D. C. Orlich, et al. (1994) provided a tested model that shows how teachers can use questioning, small group discussions, and inquiry in a most humane manner and yet meet the conditions of constructivist learning. In addition, this general model has had one successful pilot project in the state. Twenty teachers in the Lassen Educational Service District evaluated this model in 1994 as being most usable and relevant to science teaching and meeting the state's Science Framework.

References

Batey, A., and S. Hart-Landsberg. (1993). *Riding the Wind.* Portland: Northwest Regional Educational Laboratory. A final report on "Rural Leadership in Science Mathematics Education."

Cobb, P., E. Yackel, and T. Wood. (1992). "A Constructivist Alternative to the Representational View of Mind in Mathematics Education." *Journal for Research in Mathematics Education,* 23, 1:2-33.

Gardner, H. (1983). *Frames of Mind: The Theory of Multiple Intelligences.* New York: Basic Books.

Orlich, D. C., et al. (1994). *Teaching Strategies: A Guide to Better Instruction*, 4th ed. Lexington, Mass.: D.C. Heath.

Vygotsky, L. (1962). *Thought and Language.* Cambridge, Mass.: M.I.T. Press.

6.   Program Personnel

Below is a listing of personnel, their duties, and responsibilities in the project.

Harvey Chandler, Project Co-Director. Chandler is the Director of the Science Improvement Center at NSU. He has developed and demonstrated STS projects working with different cultures in the state and internationally. He will: (1) aid in planning, organizing and coordinating the project; (2) be responsible for fiscal commitments through NSU's business offices; (3) be liaison with the school districts; (4) assist in teaching the STS model; (5) conduct follow-up activities during first quarter 1995-96 academic year; and (6) prepare the final report.

David Lawrence, Project Co-Director. Lawrence is an associate professor at NSU. He is the President of the state science teachers association and is very active in teacher education. He is a geologist and has been involved in numerous teacher workshops using the constructivist model. He will: (1) coordinate and illustrate teaching geology in an interactive model using water quality as the common theme; (2) assist in curriculum design; and (3) help with safety instruction.

Charles Judd, Professor of Science Instruction at NSU. He will: (1) evaluate the workshop and follow-up activities; (2) provide models illustrating constructivist, inquiry, and assessment techniques; and (3) help prepare the final report.

Lance Rodgers, Science Department Chair, Live Oak High School. He has a BS and MS in geology and industrial experience in hydrology. He will serve as a water chemistry resource person and also follow-up as noted in the proposal.

N. D. Sanchez, Supervisor of Instructional Technology at the LESD. He has taught science in the public schools for over 30 years. He will supervise and instruct the appropriate use of instructional technology in an integrated STS program.

Christine Jones, Project Assistant. She has had extensive experience assisting the conduct of science education projects at NSU since 1989. She will be responsible for secretarial/technical assistance to the project throughout the funding period.

Bart Hixon, Science Supervisor, Lassen Educational School District, Susanville. He will coordinate the dissemination of the LESD project with North teachers.

Betty McDonald, Native American Science Teacher, Colusa School District. She will provide instruction in teaching science to minority students and will be a resource specialist as noted in the proposal.

7. **Other Program Resources**

The project codirectors will secure all necessary buildings and facilities. The site scheduled for this project is Redding as it is central to the area.

The Redding School District will provide all necessary buildings and laboratory facilities. The study site scheduled for this project is the Redding geographic area as it has adequate housing and is adjacent to many potential test sites. NSU will provide, at no cost to the project, all of the "large" water quality test kits for laboratory analysis. Each "research team" will perform its own testing and during the follow-up years, each teacher will have an opportunity to utilize test kits at his/her own school at no cost. Federal agencies, for example, the U.S. Army Corps of Engineers and Fish and Wildlife Service have offered their resources.

The Lassen Peak Consortium has endorsed the linking of rural teachers into a sharing network.

Area private school teachers have a history of participating in state and federally funded staff development programs in science with the rural schools. Science teachers in these schools will be invited to participate.

8. **Program Administration**

As was noted in Section Six, the project has two codirectors. Harvey Chandler will direct major project activities. All administrative activities have been divided so that supervision, monitoring, and evaluation are distributed in a logical manner. Chandler will coordinate budgetary aspects of the project emanating from NSU. David Lawrence will coordinate all personnel who participate in the project and will work closely with Chandler in the administration of the project. Each has had significant experience in conducting and directing science education projects.

N.D. Sanchez will coordinate all technology aspects (computer networking) of the proposed project.

9. **Institutional Capacity**

North State University has identified science education as a top priority. This is reflected by the efforts in working to enhance elementary science education. However, the needs assessment and focus group of October 1994 strongly supported an extension of services to the middle and high school levels. Secondary teachers (and administrators) strongly supported the extension and dissemination of the successful 1994 LESD model into this project to encompass middle and secondary teachers. The NSU group has the resources of its institution to be marshaled to help this project be successful.

North State University is known nationally for its science education efforts. Harvey Chandler is the Director of the institutionally supported Science Improvement Center. He is an immediate past president of the state science teachers association and has had multicultural experience in the Philippines, Japan, Malaysia, and Thailand. Chandler has codirected three very successful school district projects in science education between 1988 and 1994.

David Lawrence is known nationally for his research in geology and reform efforts in science education, K-16. He has been an award-winning teacher at both the state and national levels. He is currently president of the state science teachers association. He has codirected several science education projects.

Charles Judd is very active in science education and has had extensive experience working with science teachers in rural areas and serves on two national boards for curriculum projects. He was a coordinator for the innovative and federally-funded "Project Smart," which focused on very rural science teachers from 1991-93. Judd has published on science evaluation and has evaluated science projects since 1971.

10. **Program Evaluation**
The project evaluation has three components.

1. **Workshop evaluation**. Several evaluative instruments will be used to measure participant reactions to the summer training phases. Our model is designed to provide feedback to the project staff. Content evaluations and process evaluations will be administered to allow for immediate adjustments. This procedure has been used successfully and a longitudinal study by Judd showed the model to be highly stable—even over a 21-year period.

2. **Teachers' instruction**. The second component will be to establish a baseline on science teaching strategies. Teachers will be asked to complete baseline data. Specific information will include

a. Amount of time teaching science.
b. Questioning strategies used.
c. Inquiry techniques used (constructivist model).
d. Student time-on-task for science.
e. Teacher and student talk during science periods.

During the spring of 1996, Judd will seek the above information and compare findings with the baseline data and prepare a report for the State Eisenhower Program Officer (SEPO).

3. **Pupil evaluations**. Pupil science attitudes scales will be prepared to determine the affective dimensions of the project on students. An instrument will be constructed under the direction of Judd and administered in fall 1995 and spring 1996. Data will be shared with SEPO.

11. Program Continuation

As the science and training model is field tested, it will become an important factor in the K-12 science, mathematics, and technology programs for the area schools. This project could have a major impact on the direction that science education will take at NSU. This will be the model to take school districts into the 21st Century and help meet the Goals of America 2000! The establishment of a formal network of educators will ensure continued sharing and developing of ideas.

Eisenhower Budget Summary

INSTITUTION	PROJECT DIRECTOR
North State University	Harvey Chandler
TITLE OF PROJECT	**FINANCIAL/BUDGET OFFICE CONTACT**
North State Rural Science Project	Office of Grant & Research Development

				OTHER FUNDS	PROPOSED EISENHOWER GRANT
1. PERSONNEL	**Eisenhower Funded Mos.**				
Key Personnel Salaries (Faculty, Administration)	Acad.	Sum.	Cal.		
A. Salaries I. H. Chandler		.5			
II. D. Lawrence		.5			
III. C. Judd		.23			
IV.					
B. Fringe Benefits (26%) # benefits @ 9%					
Support Personnel (Clerical, Grad, Assistants)					
A. Salaries					
I. Tech Asst. II, 155 hrs @ $16/Hr					2,480
II.					
III.					
IV.					
B. Fringe Benefits (16%)					
TOTAL PERSONNEL COSTS					
2. PARTICIPANT COSTS					
A. Tuition					
B. Fees					
C. Books					
D. Materials					
E. Travel					3,000
F. Room and Board					5,808
G. Other: Stipend $125 x 25 = $3,125; 100 x 25 x 2=$5,000					8,125
TOTAL PARTICIPANT COSTS					16,933
3. OTHER TRAVEL					
A. Mileage (Institute and Site Visits)					280
B. State Per Diem					1,254
4. SUPPLIES					
A. Kit Materials, Demo Project Supplies, Phone, Mailing					2,000
B.					
5. EQUIPMENT RENTAL					
A. Four telephone lines in Redding for computer linkage.					500
B.					
6. CONTRACTUAL					
A. Hixon, McDonald, Sanchez					3,141
B. Teachers—Two Teachers					1,098
7. OTHER					
A.					
B.					
C.					
8.	**TOTAL DIRECT COSTS (Sum of Items 1-7)**				
9.	**INDIRECT COSTS (@ 8%) (Sum of Item 8)**				
10.	**TOTAL COSTS (Sum of Items 8 & 9)**				

North State Rural Science Project
Budget Narrative Detail

1. Personnel

All NSU personnel are paid as per established salary.

Key Personnel Salaries (Faculty, Administration)

1. H. Chandler	.5 month @ $_____/mo	$_____
2. D. Lawrence	.5 month @ $_____/mo	$_____
3. C. Judd	.23 month @ $_____/mo	$_____

Fringe Benefits

26% for #1 and 2 $_____   9% for #3 $_____ $_____

Support Personnel Salaries

A. Tech Asst. II; 155 hrs @ $16 per hour $ 2,480

B. Fringe Benefits (16%) $_____

Total Personnel Costs $_____

2. Participant Costs

E. Travel (Mileage)

SUMMER INSTITUTE: Each participant will receive an average of $40.

25 participants x $40 $ 1,000

FALL AND SPRING FOLLOW-UPS: Each participant will receive an average of $40.

25 participants x $40 x 2 follow-ups $ 2,000

F. Room and Board

SUMMER INSTITUTE: 22 participants will receive lodging and meals at $66 per diem.

$66 per diem x 22 participants x 4 nights $ 5,808

G. Other (Stipends)

SUMMER INSTITUTE: $125 per participant.

$125 x 25 participants $ 3,125

FALL AND SPRING FOLLOW-UPS: $100 per participant.

$100 X 25 participants x 2 follow-ups $ 5,000

TOTAL PARTICIPANTS COSTS   <u>**$16,933**</u>

3. Other Travel

A. Mileage

SUMMER INSTITUTE: Chandler and Judd from Sonoma/Chico one round trip (228 pt. to pt.; 22 vicinity)

250 miles @ .28/mile $ 70

Lawrence from Sonoma/Chico one round trip (228 pt. to pt.; 22 vicinity)

250 miles @ .28/mile $ 70

SITE VISITS AND FOLLOW UP

2 days total—Chandler and Judd

Mileage: $70/each trip $ 140

(continued)

B. Lodging

SUMMER INSTITUTE

$66/day for Chandler (5), Lawrence (5), Judd (5)

$66 x 5 = $330 x 3 $ 990

SITE VISITS AND FOLLOW-UP

Site visits plus spring follow-up, Redding

Chandler (2), Judd (2)

Per Diem $66 x 2 days x 2 $ 264

TOTAL OTHER TRAVEL COSTS $ 1,534

4. Supplies

Included are expandable costs and materials for teachers to
"take home" for demonstration purposes, long distance
telephone, faxing, mail services, reproduction of print material,
and project supplies and kits for teachers. $ 2,000

TOTAL SUPPLIES $ 2,000

5. Equipment Rental

Four telephone lines in Redding for computer linkage. $ 500

TOTAL EQUIPMENT RENTAL $ 500

6. Contractual (Consultants)

Bart Hixon	2 days @ $250/day	$ 500
Mileage	350 miles @ .28/mi	98
Per Diem	2 days x $66	132
N. D. Sanchez	4 days @ $250/day	$ 1,000
Mileage	350 miles @ .28/mi	98
Per Diem	4 days x $66	264
Betty McDonald	2 days @ $250	$ 500
Teacher follow-up	3 days @ $150	450
Travel Average	$25 x 3 days	75
Meal Allowance	$8 x 3 days	24
Two Teachers		
Follow-up for 3 days		
Stipend	$150/day x 2 x 3 days	$ 900
Travel	Average $25 x 2 x 3 days	150
Meal Allowance	$8 x 2 x 3 days	48

TOTAL CONSULTANT COSTS $ 4,239

7. Other (N/A)

8. Total Direct Costs (Sum of Items 1-7)

9. Indirect Costs (@ 8%) (Sum of Item 8)

10. Total Costs (sum of Items 8 & 9)

NOTE: Indirect cost rate is fixed at 8 percent.

References

Bloom, B.S. (1984). "The 2 Sigma Problem: The Search for Methods of Group Instruction as Effective as One-to-One Tutoring." *Educational Researcher* 13, 6: 4–16.

Cohen, J. (1988). *Statistical Power Analysis for the Behavioral Sciences*, 2nd Ed. Hillsdale, N.J.: Lawrence Erlbaum Associates.

Cook, D.L. (1978). *Program Evaluation and Review Technique.* Lanham, Md.: University Press of America, Inc.

Eisner, E.W. (March 1984). "Can Educational Research Inform Educational Practice?" *Phi Delta Kappan* 65, 7: 447–452.

Fyechtling, J., ed. (1994). *User-Friendly Handbook for Project Evaluation: Science, Mathematics, Engineering and Technology Education.* Arlington, Va.: Directorate for Education and Human Resources, National Science Foundation.

Glaser, R. (1963). "Instructional Technology and the Measurement of Learning Outcomes: Some Questions." *American Psychologist* 18: 519–521.

Glass, G.V. (1976). "Primary Secondary and Meta Analysis of Research." *Educational Researcher* 5, 11: 3–8.

Glass, G.V. (1980). "Summarizing Effect Sizes." In *New Directions for Methodology of Social and Behavioral Science: Quantitative Assessment of Research Domain*, edited by R. Rosenthal. San Francisco: Jossey-Bass.

Gulick, L.H., and L. F. Urwick. (1937). *Papers on the Science of Administration.* New York: Columbia University.

Helmer, O. (1967). *Analysis of the Future: The Delphi Method.* Santa Monica, Calif.: Rand Corporation.

House, E.R. (1978). "Assumptions Underlying Evaluation Models." *Educational Researcher* 7, 3: 4–12.

Kelly, T.F. (1991). *Practical Strategies for School Improvement.* Wheeling, Ill.: National School Services.

Orlich, D.C. (1987). *Findings From In-Service Education Research for Elementary Science Teaching.* Washington, D.C.: Council for Elementary Science International, Monograph and Occasional Paper Series, No. 2, National Science Teachers Association.

Scriven, M. (1967). *The Methodology of Evaluation.* AERA Monograph Series on Curriculum Evaluation, No. 1: 39–83.

Walberg, H.J. (1991). "Productive Teaching and Instruction: Assessing the Knowledge Base." In *Effective Teaching: Current Research*, edited by H.C. Waxman and H.J. Walberg. Berkeley, Calif.: McCutchan Publishing Corporation, for the National Society for the Study of Education.

The Author

Donald C. Orlich is Professor of Education and Science Instruction at Washington State University, Science Mathematics Engineering Education Center, Pullman, Washington 99164-4237; telephone: (509) 335-4844, fax: (509) 335-7389.